my son, my son

Bernard Palmer

WHOLESOME READING DISTRIBUTED BY:
CHOICE BOOKS
RT. #1 IRWIN, OHIO 43029
We Welcome Your Response

Moody Press, Chicago

Moody Paperback Edition, 1973

ISBN: 0-8024-5661-8

Printed in the United States of America

FOREWORD

We first felt constrained to write an article for *Christian Life* magazine, setting down our experience with our son, Barry. The response of that article was so overwhelming that we were asked to enlarge the material into a novel.

My Son, My Son is the result.

The book was not easy to conceive or write; or was it easy for my wife and daughter-in-law to have it written. Certain facts have been changed to protect those who were caught in the vortex of our problem for no fault of their own, but basically the story is true. It lays bare the dread and heartache and unspeakable joy that we have experienced.

We have written this book in the hope that it will be of help and encouragement to others who are faced with the same situation. If that is true, we will have reward enough for our efforts.

BERNARD PALMER

This book is dedicated to our daughter-in-law, Kathryn, and her three lovely children, Lori, Juli and Jim Palmer, who graciously sacrificed their own privacy that others might be helped.

1

ROYCE LAWSON, bare feet tingling on the cold floor, remained at the telephone momentarily, clutching the dead instrument with a trembling hand. It wasn't true. It couldn't be. He only dreamed that the phone had rung and that he had gone to answer it. He would waken soon and realize that he was still in bed, the victim of his own troubled mind.

"Royce," Penny called from their bedroom. "Who was it? What did they want?"

The familiar sound of her voice jerked him back to reality. He rubbed a stubby hand across his broad face and fumbled the phone back to its cradle. As he did so he swayed slightly and reached out with an unsteady hand to catch himself.

"Royce," Penny said once more, "who was it?"

He did not answer her. For half a minute he was as motionless as though sculptured of marble. Then, finding strength, he stumbled across the floor to the big chair before the fireplace. Without fully realizing what he was doing, he groped for the chair in the semidarkness and lowered himself into it.

His silence to Penny's question was not like him. They had no secrets from each other. But he had to have time to think—to weigh the dreadful news the early morning call had brought.

Darkness cradled the Lawsons' long living room with tender hands. Skillfully it wove the shadows to hide the bare areas in the red mohair of the divan and camouflaged the worn traffic patterns in the cotton carpet that had been bought when the house was new.

But for all of its well-used furnishings and haphazard decor, the Lawson home was warm and vibrant—a gay, living thing that attracted others irresistibly.

For some reason the kids of the neighborhood looked on it as their own. Some of them were always there, researching a paper from a book the library didn't have, playing ping-pong in the basement, or talking seriously with Penny or Royce about a real or fancied problem.

Meals in the Lawson home were usually tumultuous. Penny seldom knew how many would be eating with them until time to set the table. Then her guests of the afternoon, both boys and girls, would phone home for permission to stay from bewildered, often hurt mothers.

"I can't understand why my kids always want to be at your place," Penny's friends would say.

At first having them around bothered Penny, but she soon learned to order her young guests about the way she did her own family and they loved her for it.

"Sue, help Becky set the table, will you?" she would ask, as though Sue was her own daughter.

"You may stay for dinner, Bob, but you'll have to help the twins with the dishes, OK?"

Royce didn't mind either the inflated grocery bills or the noise. He didn't enter into the conversation as freely as Penny did. It wasn't his way. But when he got acquainted he kidded their young guests constantly.

"Your dad isn't like mine, Becky," they would say to his daughter. "He teases all the time."

"I can't understand him," she would answer, frustration mingling with the pride in her voice. "We don't do things like ordinary people do, and he never seems to see that we need new furniture; but he'll buy us an $18 book we don't even ask for."

"Or take us to Chicago with him on the plane when he's got to go there on business," Ned, one of the twins added, "so we can see a major league ball game."

But, though the house reverberated with gay young laughter during the day and early evening, it darkened and fell asleep after the ten o'clock news. The chances were that by that hour Becky would be in her room at the end of the hall after washing her hair and putting it up twice before it suited her suddenly critical taste. And Ned and Tom were in the basement room they shared with a bevy of model planes and cars. The porch light Penny had insisted on leaving lighted still fought valiantly against the darkness. It was a feeble thing, one of Royce's periodic efforts at economizing, but it was large enough to chase the darkness from the door.

A car rattled by, shaking the night.

The graying architect, sitting alone in the big chair before the fireplace, started at the sudden sound. He jerked himself erect and spun to face the door.

The car squealed its defiance on the corner and went roaring away as Craig did so often. The deep-throated snarl of the motor hurried into the distance, leaving the night as silent and desolate as before.

Royce supported his weight with a hand on either arm of the big chair, ears tuned to the breathless hush of the early morning hours.

At first it seemed to him that Craig must surely have been the driver of that car; that he would roar up the street three or four blocks, spin the vehicle in a careening U-turn and come keening back into the drive like a thing berserk, throwing gravel as he jammed the brakes. A moment's hesitation after the engine was shut off, the noisy slamming of a car door, and he would hear those familiar footsteps approaching the house.

But it wasn't Craig. Their son wouldn't be coming home. Sweat pearled Royce's forehead and he wiped it away with a quivering hand.

This should have been no surprise to him, this thing he

7

had been called about. He had known it was going to happen some time, although God knew he had prayed that it wouldn't. But he had known, even as he tried to close his eyes to it. Not that he hadn't tried to mask his concern from Penny.

"Craig's pretty much like all the other kids his age," he would tell her, "except that he's a little more daring than the rest. And that gets him into more trouble in the classroom than he would get into otherwise."

"He's a good boy," she would answer loyally.

But all the while they both had known that there was a wild streak deep within their oldest son—a surly defiance that whispered darkly of trouble to come. And when Craig was old enough to go out at night Royce was never at ease until he returned home again. And even then that nagging doubt persisted. Where had his son gone? Whom had he been with? What had they done?

And, should the phone ring at night, he jumped out of bed, trembling violently, to answer it.

Now the phone call had come with the message he had been dreading.

Royce was glad Rita had not lived to see it. At least she was spared that heartache. It would have killed her to know what had happened to the son she gave her life to bring into the world. She had always been so gentle, so kind, so concerned that her life be above reproach. He leaned forward, clenching his fists in anguish.

He had been so lost in his own gloom that he had not heard Penny steal up quietly behind him, as though afraid she might disturb him. He didn't even know she was in the living room until she laid her hands tenderly on his shoulders.

"Penny." His voice broke.

She said nothing for the moment, but even her silence spoke to him, telling him that she shared his agony. He leaned back and grasped her tiny fingers with his own broad, stubby hands. In desperation he clung to her.

"They've got Craig." The voice didn't sound like his at

8

all. It was wooden, expressionless, as though the life had suddenly fled its owner.

"What did they say?"

"They—" He tried to tell her, but his throat choked.

Impulsively Penny bent and kissed him on the forehead. He tightened his grasp of her hands and pulled her closer to him. There was strength and courage for him in her nearness.

"Craig was arrested tonight."

Her muscles spasmed, jerking her slight frame violently. Without looking at her Royce knew there would be no color in her cheeks—that her eyes would be round and staring.

"I wish there was some way of making this easier," he said flatly, "but Craig was arrested tonight for drunken driving."

Penny gasped. She got to her feet but stood rigidly—frozen into immobility.

He wished he could stop there, but that was only half the story. There was more that had to be told to her.

"He and the Brown kid stole a car from Acme Motors."

"Oh, no!" Penny's exclamation was involuntary—almost a prayer. She swayed weakly and had to grasp the back of the chair for support.

In that moment silence gripped them in a way it had never taken hold of them before. Regardless of the circumstances, they had always been able to talk to each other, to share the joys or the hurts of any situation. They were still able to share the agony of that lonely night, but in silence, robbed of words.

The cuckoo clock on the wall behind Royce struck the hour of three in the morning. He looked back quickly, angered by the noisy intrusion. Always before he had enjoyed the pleasant sound that marked the coming and going of the half hours and the hours. The little bird was cheery and as warm and friendly as Penny's gay, impulsive laugh. Now, however, it was coarse and grating. An almost uncontrollable urge to destroy the source of the sound swept over him. He wanted to jerk the clock from the wall and smash it on the hearth.

How could it mark the hours as though everything was just as they had been a few minutes ago when time suddenly ceased to exist for him and Penny? How could he ever listen to the noisy ticking of the clock and the raucous cry of the cuckoo again?

Finally Penny spoke once more, her voice as distant as her mind.

"Did they want us to come down tonight?" she asked.

A long, tearing sigh escaped from the confines of his heart.

"The sheriff, Joe Christy, said that Craig wants to see me right away, but—" It was hard to go on. Hard to repeat those things that rubbed his nerve ends raw. "But Joe thought it would be better if we waited. He said Craig would be in better condition to talk to us in the morning."

She took the information without comment, numbly, as though it was impossible for her to be hurt more. Royce glanced quickly at her.

"What did we do wrong, Penny?" he asked miserably. "Where did we fail Craig?"

She did not speak at once.

"I've been asking myself that same question," she acknowledged. "But I don't know. I just don't know."

They went to bed presently, but Royce could not sleep. The fact that he had been expecting something like this to happen did little to prepare him for the stunning blow of the phone call.

Craig was in jail. Craig, his son, locked in a narrow cell alone! Craig, who could never stand a locked door, even as a child. Who, before he was old enough to go to school, had insisted on being outside a while every day, regardless of the weather. For Craig to be locked up would be staggering.

And the shame of it!

The dull pain within Royce continued without letup, squeezing his chest with icy fingers. Somehow the great, numbing ache had penetrated his rib cage and was pressing

10

relentlessly against his heart. It was still there when he got up the next morning, but he didn't mention it to Penny. She had enough to think about already.

"You're going to get him out, aren't you, Daddy?" Becky asked when she heard it. "You aren't going to make him stay there."

The twins were not nearly as concerned and understanding.

"That stupe doesn't think about anybody but himself, Dad," Ned said angrily. "He got into this mess. Let him get out of it the best way he can."

"That's what I say," Tom put in with all the brash confidence of his fourteen years. "Maybe he won't be so quick to get into a jam the next time."

It hurt Royce to hear them talk that way, but he said nothing. This wasn't going to be easy for them either. A little town like Glenville was bred and weaned on gossip. By tomorrow at this time the entire family would be the chief object of discussion around the business district and from one "Population 5,255" sign to the other on the opposite side of town. Tongues would clack over the telephone. Choice exaggerations would be passed from one itching ear to another at the lunch counters frequented by some who pretended to be Royce and Penny's best friends. It had ever been thus.

Royce had long known about Glenville's gossiping. Indeed, he had entered into it himself on occasion. It was an intriguing, self-satisfying game to play. It could make a fellow feel, by comparison, at least, that he was quite successful, or brilliant, or moral as compared to his associates. And, it had seemed quite harmless. Now Royce recognized gossip for all its ugliness.

"I wish we didn't have to go down and see him there," Royce told Penny miserably. "It's not going to be easy."

"I know."

"I can go alone."

"No, Royce!" Her lips trembled. "He's my son too!"

The instant he spoke he was sorry for it. Penny had not

11

given birth to Craig, that was true, but she nursed him through his first illness, pulled his first baby tooth, and cried when he set out for school for the first time alone.

Craig had been proud of her in those days. He seemed to take particular pride in lisping the word "mother" as though, in spite of his age, he was aware of what life would be like without a mother and how fortunate he was that Penny had come to live with them.

No, Royce could not deny her the right to go along with him, as difficult as it would be for her.

The sheriff was at the station when they arrived.

"I'm sorry about this, Royce," Joe Christy said. "It was one of the toughest arrests I've ever had to make."

He showed them into a small side room where they could talk to their son alone, and sent one of the other officers to bring him.

The boy scuffed reluctantly along the narrow corridor ahead of his police escort, blood-veined eyes averted. Craig was taller than the officer by half a head, a slender, spidery individual the girls stared at when he came swaggering by. There was a handsome cut to his face, marred only by a surly mouth and smoldering defiance in his eyes, an insolence a certain type of girls found irresistibly appealing.

But now his shoulders sagged until he seemed no taller than the officer. His face was flushed and bloated and deep circles aged his eyes. The swagger and insolence were gone— at least for the moment—and there was an unnatural meekness about him.

Royce winced as he saw his oldest son, as though he had been struck in the face.

"Hello, Craig," he managed to say.

No answer.

"Hello, Craig."

Grimly the boy raised his head to stare at Penny. The old sneer twisted his mouth.

"What's *she* doing here?"

2

THE FLOWERS had been taken from the church to the cemetery at the close of the service, but to Royce the aroma was still there, permeating the sanctuary and drifting down to the basement where the family and a few close friends had gathered for lunch. He didn't think his nostrils would ever be free of it.

Mechanically Royce extended a firm young hand to those who came up to him. He listened distantly to their awkwardly murmured condolences and tried to think of something to say in response to their clumsy efforts to carry on a conversation.

He knew they meant well, but that didn't make it any easier. Why didn't they all go away and leave him alone? Why did they think they had to try to talk to him, mouthing empty words and phrases as though they could soothe.

Didn't they know what had happened?

Rita was gone. Life had ceased for her, and his life was over. Finished. He would never know what it was to laugh again.

Royce had been totally unprepared for what had happened. Even when he stood in the hospital corridor, hair disheveled and brown eyes dark with fear, and heard the attending physician describe Rita's rapidly deteriorating condition, he had refused to believe it. This couldn't be. She was too young—too gay and beautiful for her life to end. Death could not come to one so young.

Everything was going to work out somehow. It always had.

In spite of his blind refusal even to consider that Rita could be taken from him, he remained at the hospital until the supervisor sternly ordered him home.

"There has been no change in your wife's condition. You must go home now and get some rest." Her voice softened until she sounded much like his own mother who lived in southern Kansas. "I'll call you if there's any change."

It seemed that he had only time to lie down and close his eyes before the phone rang. At the first tingle of the bell he was up and half across the floor.

"Mr. Lawson?" Even the well-disciplined voice of the supervisor broke slightly. "Dr. Magnuson thinks you should come down at once."

"How is Rita?" he demanded, suddenly cold and shaken.

"The doctor wants you to come right away," she replied.

Whether Rita died before the phone call or while he was racing across town to the hospital, he didn't know. Nor did it make any difference now. She was gone. Nothing mattered anymore.

Royce went through the motions of making the funeral arrangements, but actually others had to do it for him, suggesting the answers to questions that were put to him. Even an hour after the funeral he could not remember who was playing the organ, and he wasn't sure who the soloist was. He had not been sitting where he could see the pallbearers and he could only call to mind the names of four of them, members of Rita's high school graduating class. He would have to wait until he got home and looked at the folder in his pocket to find out who the others were.

Although Royce had completed his education and worked two years as an architect he didn't look much older than when he was a senior in high school. He was still slim and straight and his curly hair was still embarrassingly unruly.

14

He had been painfully conscious of the way he looked as he stood before the mirror that morning and ran his razor over his thin cheeks.

His features were even and well formed, except for a bump on the bridge of his nose where the bone was broken by a line drive at a baseball game. Nobody, except his mother and possibly Rita, however, would have called him handsome. His wasn't that sort of a face.

In the mirror Royce saw the care-weary sag to his shoulders and, forcibly, he tried to straighten them. He wasn't going to let anyone else see his grief if he could help it. It was too profound—too sacred to have anyone else look in on it.

And, above all, he wasn't having anyone feeling sorry for him.

There was a stony set to his jaw as he came out of the bathroom that morning and a flinty gleam in his eyes. All through the day he held his emotions grimly in check. And now, standing in the church basement trying to talk to those who came up to him, a numb, bewildering apathy took hold, an apathy he was too weary to even try to understand. He dimly heard what was going on, but in a detached, indifferent way. It was as though someone else was standing there mouthing empty, meaningless words and phrases. He was off to one side, viewing the scene and hearing the conversation, but was not a part of what was going on.

After a time Royce became aware that one of his relatives was standing before him. His mother's sister, Eleanor, extended a bony hand that was heavy with diamonds. Hers was an ample, well-padded frame, tastefully clothed in a gown from one of Denver's exclusive shops. Her eyes were weak and she needed glasses, but somebody must have told her she looked better without them. She usually let them hang on the gold chain about her neck while she squinted and blinked in an effort to see what was going on around her. In poor light such as that in the church basement she was forced to put them on as much as she disliked them. Now she adjusted the glasses on the bridge of her thin, ridged nose and surveyed Royce self-consciously. He felt himself cringing under her pitying stare.

"I'm so sorry for you," she cooed, her free hand wandering up to the matched pearls of her necklace, as though calling his attention to them and the fact that they were genuine and cost as much as most men made in half a year. "I'm so sorry for you, Royce."

Her voice chilled him. For some reason she had always affected him that way. Perhaps it was because she had always had so much and his folks so little. Or, more likely, because she would never let them forget it.

He thanked her for her concern when she expressed her sympathy. But even as he spoke he didn't know for sure what he was saying. They were just words murmured at random for something to say. But it didn't matter. At such a time, regardless of who did the talking, nobody listened.

Idly Royce's mind drifted to the thin shaft of light that angled through the basement window and played on the inlaid shuffleboard court in the tile floor. He and Rita had spent more happy evenings in the church basement than anyone had a right to have, playing shuffleboard and ping-pong with the members of their couples' class.

Others would still come down to the church basement, their carefree laughter revealing the fun they were having. Perhaps they would come that very evening, ignoring the pungent aroma of the funeral flowers. But he and Rita would not be there. They could never come again.

Briefly his resentment flared. Why should life be over for them almost before it began? Why was he visited with such a tragedy?

He had forgotten about his relative momentarily, but she was still standing there, talking. Slowly the words she was speaking came into focus, clearing like the blurred image in a telescope as the lens is moved.

"When you married so young I thought, 'What a tragedy that Royce would be married so young when he could have a promising future.' Edward and I were twenty-nine when we were married. Had our own home, a car, and money in

16

the bank. Now, you're not yet twenty-nine and already you're a widower." She clucked her disapproval. "With a newborn baby to look after."

Although he was trying hard to follow her, he was only vaguely aware of what she was talking about. She must have a purpose, but he could not fathom it. Numbly he waited for her to continue.

"And what are you going to do with poor, motherless little Craig now?" she asked.

"Do with him?" he echoed. Still he did not quite understand what she was trying to find out from him. What did a man do with his son? "What do you mean, 'do with him'?" he asked.

"You won't be able to keep him, of course." She spoke firmly, decisively.

It wasn't that Royce was slow of mind, but the lethargy of shock still gripped him, and the thought of not keeping Craig was so foreign it was completely incomprehensible.

"Why wouldn't I be able to keep him?"

She allowed a smile to rest briefly on her lips before sweeping it away.

"You don't have anyone to take care of him, for one thing."

"I'll get someone."

"For another, you'll get married again before long."

He staggered as though she had slapped him.

"The young ones always do," she continued before he recovered enough to protest. "And when you get another wife, she won't want Rita's baby. Especially after she has babies of her own."

He stared at her narrowly. These things she was saying weren't true; they couldn't be true. No one could ever take Rita's place. If he lived to be an old man, he would spend the rest of his life alone. And as for Craig, he could find someone to take care of him. He didn't know who, but he'd find somebody. He had already lost Rita; he wasn't going to lose her baby too.

"If you'll let Edward and me adopt him," she was saying,

setting down her conditions crisply, as though she was making an offer on a piece of property, "we'll take care of him for you."

Anger smoked in his sad eyes.

"I'll manage, thank you."

She seemed surprised at his refusal.

"We'll be able to give him a good home."

"He has a good home."

Her mouth tightened. Disappointment gleamed in her eyes and for an instant they were soft and luminous behind the thick lenses. Royce couldn't help feeling sorry for her. She and Edward were so alone.

"Well," she said with some reluctance, "if you do change your mind, Royce, you can let us know."

Rita's aunt was to come to him about the same matter later that afternoon, as he was sitting alone, a cup of coffee in his hand. She crossed the room and sat down beside him. About the same age as his own Aunt Eleanor, she was a gentle, gray-haired, motherly person whose eyes gleamed as she talked. She had no children of her own, but had taken in several for varying periods, including Rita when her mother was ill for two long years. She had been a second mother to his wife.

"I've been wanting to talk with you, Royce," she said, pushing aside her own grief. "I don't know what you're going to do with that sweet baby of yours, but if you find it difficult to take care of him, or if you need a little help for a while, our home is always open. I want you to know that."

He took her hand between his own with a tenderness he hadn't even known he felt toward her.

"Thank you," he said quietly. "You don't know how much I appreciate that."

The baby had remained at the hospital until after the funeral. The next day Aunt Sally went with Royce to get him. They took him home in the brightly decorated bassinette Rita had fixed for him in those last few happy days at home. He could scarcely bring himself to look at it.

At first Aunt Sally thought it would be easier to take the baby into her own home, but when she saw the loneliness in Royce' eyes she decided against it.

"I'll come over and stay with you until you find a housekeeper," she told him.

"That shouldn't be too long. I'm running an ad in tomorrow night's paper."

Finding someone to come in and take care of Craig was more of a problem than he anticipated. The matter of propriety was limiting, in itself. He couldn't have anyone within twenty years of his own age.

"It just wouldn't look right," he was informed by wellmeaning individuals who were serving notice on him that he would have to be careful or he would sacrifice much of his own reputation.

A housekeeper the community of Glenville would accept without lifted eyebrows and clacking tongues had to be a motherly type, preferably a widow with grown children, somewhat frowzy and with hair liberally sprinkled with gray. It would help if she had known Rita or was acquainted with her parents.

The first two nights the ad appeared there was no response to it. He was beginning to get concerned that he would be unable to get anyone when Martha Laird phoned.

"You're the party who wants a housekeeper?" she asked.

"That's right." He could scarcely believe she was applying for the position, that he might be able to get somebody to come in and keep up the house and look after Craig.

Aunt Sally came to the kitchen door and he signaled her the good news with his thumb and forefinger.

"If you'll give me your name and address," he said, making no attempt to conceal his excitement, "I'll come right over to see you."

The voice on the wire froze him.

"That won't be necessary," she retorted crisply. "I will come to your home. I would want to have a look at it before I make my decision anyway."

"That's fine. You can come over anytime."

She paused hesitantly.

"I must ask one question before I come, Mr. Lawson."

"Sure. Go ahead."

"If I should come over at 8 o'clock this evening would—would we be properly chaperoned?"

His lower jaw sagged.

"I suppose so. I mean, yes, Aunt Sally will be here. She's taking care of the baby now."

Precisely at 8 o'clock the doorbell rang and Royce bounced to open it. A gaunt, angular woman stood in the doorway, a pinched autumn hat of uncertain age or origin perched atop her sparse graying hair. The reflected rays of the lamp near the door deepened the shadows beneath her eyes, but did nothing to round the sharp lines of her cheekbones or the squareness of her jaw.

For an instant Royce stared at her.

"How do you do," she said in that same crisp, no-nonsense voice that had addressed him on the phone earlier in the evening.

"Oh—" He shook himself back to reality. "Oh, I'm sorry. Won't you come in?"

The invitation was of no effect. She had already stepped into the living room and was surveying it with practiced, expressionless eyes.

"I'm Royce Lawson," he said, thrusting out his hand.

She ignored it pointedly.

"And this is Mrs. Sally Olson. She's the one I was telling you about who has been keeping house for me and taking care of the baby until I can get someone else."

The newcomer greeted Aunt Sally with a bleak smile.

"I'm glad to know you."

At Royce's invitation to sit down she unbuttoned her coat, pushed it back with a twist of her shoulders and lowered herself to a chair. The chair she chose was hard and straight-backed. As she sat there, both feet planted firmly on the floor and her hands clasped on her lap, she gave the appearance of an austere third-grade teacher about to question one of her slower pupils.

For a time silence stood between them, as though grasped by invisible hands that had caught it and would not let it go.

Royce studied the stern figure before him. There was a plain gold band on the third finger of his guest's left hand. That meant she had been married. Her husband had undoubtedly died several years before. As far as meeting the dictates of propriety was concerned, he didn't anticipate any problems if he was able to hire her. Even the loosest tongues in Glenville would find gossip about Mrs. Laird unthinkable. That suited him too. He didn't care to run the risk of being talked about.

At last the silence grew unbearable. Royce cleared his throat.

"Did you see my ad in the paper?" he began.

She inclined her chin slightly in an almost imperceptible nod.

"I have been taking care of an elderly woman until she passed away two weeks ago," she said. "I could have gone right to work at several other places, but I wanted to have a little rest first."

"I see."

He was trying to decide what to say to her first. He had never hired anyone before and didn't know exactly how to begin. He supposed he ought to ask her about other jobs she had held and names and addresses of references, but he was afraid to do that. She might misunderstand his intentions and flounce out of the house, leaving him without help at all.

His main concern was the amount of money she would expect. A young architect didn't make too much and they hadn't had either hospitalization or life insurance on Rita. They had squirreled away a few hundred dollars to pay the expenses of Craig's birth but that had disappeared in the first flurry of tests and the consultation with the specialist. He had some sizable bills to pay.

Mrs. Laird would probably decide she couldn't come when she learned what wages he could afford to pay, he told himself.

But his visitor soon relieved him of the responsibility of questioning her.

"I am fifty-four years old," she informed him. "My husband died eleven years ago and we have no children. I've been supporting myself doing housekeeping and working as a practical nurse. Here are my references."

She handed him a small sheaf of envelopes.

"Thank you."

He opened one and started to look at it.

"You can read them at your leisure when I'm gone," she informed him.

"Oh—oh, yes." Sheepishly he put the letter back in the envelope.

"I don't know you, Mr. Lawson," she continued, "so I, too, must ask some questions."

She wanted to know if he smoked or drank, if he entertained often, and if he was accustomed to keeping late hours.

"I'm not as young as I used to be," she informed him, "and I must have my rest."

He was glad the questions were no more difficult. He didn't smoke or drink, although he couldn't see how that could matter to her one way or the other. And as far as entertaining was concerned, that was unthinkable. He wouldn't be entertaining now that Rita was gone.

His answers must have satisfied her. A faint smile of approval flecked her lips for the first time since she entered the house.

Finally there was only the matter of wages to be discussed and that could be put off no longer. It had to be brought out in the open.

"I'm afraid I won't be able to pay you very much," he said fearfully, mentioning a figure.

The corners of her mouth tightened.

"I have been getting considerably more than that," she said.

His heart fell.

"But I like to be where I'm needed."

His eyes widened. Martha Laird was so austere—so demanding. It was incredible that she would work for anyone for less than the going wage. But that was the way it sounded unless he had mistaken the meaning of her statement.

"Do I take it that you—you will come and work for me for the wage I mentioned?" he asked.

Briefly her carefully nurtured guard came down and the harsh glint in her eyes softened.

"I saw your ad in the paper three days ago," she confessed, "and I haven't been able to sleep since, just thinking about that poor, motherless little one of yours with no one to take care of him."

Before she left she agreed to start work the following Monday morning. Her references lay unopened and unread on the end table.

Thoughtfully he turned back to the kitchen when Mrs. Laird was gone.

"What do you think of her, Aunt Sally?" he asked.

She finished filling the final bottle of formula, screwed the cap securely in place and set it in the refrigerator, ready for the night feedings.

"I think she will be very efficient, Royce," she said.

3

HAVING MRS. LAIRD in the home was not like having Aunt Sally there, Royce decided. He missed those long talks they had in the kitchen after the baby had been fed and put to sleep. He missed having someone around who didn't mind if he talked about Rita or who didn't change the subject if he did chance to mention her. He missed being able to talk with someone who loved his wife and missed her almost as much as he did. There was no one quite like Aunt Sally. It was not to Mrs. Laird's discredit that she could not measure up to her.

The gray-haired housekeeper proved to be extremely capable. She may not have raised any children of her own, but she took care of the baby with calm efficiency. From the very first morning on the job Royce knew that his son was in competent, well-trained hands. That was one problem he could completely dismiss from his mind.

Making the adjustment to Rita's death was another matter. Mercifully, a certain numbness still dulled his mind. He went mechanically through the motions of living, going to the office each morning, coming home at night and holding the baby for a while before the little one had to go to bed. Those first few weeks he seemed able to will himself not to think—to blot out the aching memories of Rita for hours at a time.

Gradually, however, the shock wore off, leaving his nerves frayed and raw, the ache in his heart unhealed. It was then, in helpless desperation, that grief and remorse for real or fancied wrongs surged back upon him.

Somehow he was able to quit thinking about Rita long enough during the day to do his work with a certain degree of efficiency. It was the nights that were torturous.

Always when he came home after a day's work she had been waiting for him with a smile on her lips, even when she was heavy with Craig and so sick she was miserable. They had dinner together, just the two of them, listening to the news on the radio. Afterward they went for a walk or sat and read, or went to a party at the church. Occasionally they went visiting or had guests in. They weren't the kind who had to be doing something constantly in order to be happy. They found enjoyment enough just in being together.

Now there was only emptiness in the little house that had been so happy a few short months before. To be sure, Mrs. Laird was there, but she was like a necessary piece of furniture. She seldom talked to him except when she needed something. And there was the baby who had a pair of lungs like an auctioneer when he was uncomfortable or just unhappy. But home wasn't the same. It would never be the same again.

A great loneliness took hold of Royce in those days and weeks—a loneliness that would not let him sleep at night. No one had ever seen him cry during that period, but there were mornings when he turned his pillow over and made his own bed to keep Mrs. Laird from seeing the moisture of his tears.

At first his friends had been careful to invite him over for dinner or include him in their plans in an effort to help him fight against his loneliness. But he soon discovered that the entire social system of the people he and Rita ran around with was set up by couples. Whatever they did, whether it was bowling or playing shuffleboard, was done by twos. Even the tables looked unbalanced with an odd plate stuck in someplace. Having an extra person threw everything out of kilter. And to invite an extra girl for him was too much like matchmaking. He soon grew accustomed to being excluded.

When Martha Laird first came to keep house for him Royce thought he would be fortunate to be able to keep her a few months. He was sure that she would soon get a better offer somewhere else and he would be faced with the problem of finding another housekeeper. Although she was harsh and demanding at times, he dreaded the day when she would leave. It would not be easy to find anyone to take her place, especially with Craig.

She seemed to love his son as deeply as Royce did, and Craig looked on her as he would have looked upon Rita, had she lived. Martha insisted that he go to bed at a regular time every night, when Royce would have been inclined to let him stay up for a while if he wanted to. She saw that he had the proper foods to eat and that he took his vitamin supplement every morning. She comforted him when he was sad and tearful, and scolded him when he was naughty.

Under Mrs. Laird's careful eye Craig learned to crawl and later to take his first stumbling steps. She had stood by proudly when he lurched across the carpet to Royce for the first time on wobbly uncertain legs, and reminded him to show his daddy his new tooth.

She was good with Craig, there was no doubt about that. He didn't think it would have been possible for him to find anyone who would equal her in that department. If she was unpleasant for him to be around, he would have to ignore that.

The days and weeks and months dragged on endlessly for Royce in a deadly, monotonous routine. During the day he had his work to keep his mind occupied. It was still the nights that were difficult. He had no place to go where he really felt welcome, and no one to associate with except Craig and Mrs. Laird.

His son helped him a great deal during that period. The little fellow lived for the time when Royce would come back to the house. He seemed to have a sort of built-in clock that sounded an inner alarm to mark his dad's return. He would start watching the window and, as soon as Royce's car stopped at the curb, he was at the door, eyes dancing with excitement.

Craig was a bit slower than the average in learning to talk, but by the time he was two years old he was beginning to say a few words. Mrs. Laird taught him to call her mommy until Royce put a stop to it.

"I can't see the harm," the gaunt, bony woman told him indignantly. "After all, he's just a baby and he should have someone he can call 'mother.' "

"Maybe there isn't any harm to it," Royce retorted. "But I don't want it to happen again."

Mrs. Laird grumbled about the matter for two or three days, but Royce did not have to mention it to her again. She taught Craig to call her "Auntie Martha" instead.

She did not approve of the way Royce snatched his son up and held him at arm's length above his head, or wrestled with him on the floor. Not that she voiced her disapproval. She had other ways of showing it—in the set of her jaw as she worked about the kitchen, or in the way she stormed noisily across the floor.

In spite of Craig and Mrs. Lawson, Royce's loneliness increased. If only there was someone he could talk to—someone who would listen to what he had to say, and understand. He had never before considered remarriage. Even now shame whipped him as the thought came sneaking in. Didn't he know that he couldn't remarry? he asked himself. That would be betraying Rita and make a mockery of the love they had for each other.

Still, he was so lonely. So very lonely.

Before that time he hadn't even thought about going out with anyone. Now, however, the matter did come to mind. There was no one he could talk with about it. It would be too embarrassing to let even a close friend see into that corner of his heart. But he did something he had never done before. He prayed about it.

He and Rita had always prayed together, locked in each

27

other's arms, before they went to sleep. Since her death he had continued to pray more or less mechanically. His prayers were general and repetitious, asking God to watch over Craig and his parents and to help him with his work. Since his prayers for Rita's life had been unanswered, he had never quite dared to nail down his requests to anything specific.

Now, although somewhat timidly, he began to ask God to send someone his way who could love both him and Craig. But that had been six months before and nothing happened. He hadn't been at all sure that praying would change the situation. He wasn't even sure he was supposed to go with anyone else, or even to think about remarriage. He knew that the marriage vows were binding only until the death of one partner or the other, but perhaps his lot was to remain single and devote his life to raising Craig. If that was the way it was to be, he could manage somehow. Since Rita's death he no longer permitted himself to believe that he couldn't take any given situation, or that he, as some favored creature, would not be expected to walk a hard road. But the prospect of spending the rest of his life alone made the years stretch ahead bleak and desolate.

At times he sat in his office, or lay in bed, staring up at the ceiling. Idly he thought about the various girls he knew. They were nice enough, he supposed. Especially the girls from church. Almost any of them would make a suitable wife for somebody. But he couldn't see himself getting interested in any of them. He couldn't imagine any of them taking Craig and raising him as her own.

Royce had pushed the matter to the far reaches of his mind where it lay all but forgotten. That was the situation when Aunt Sally phoned and invited him to a family picnic that evening.

"We completely forgot to get in touch with you until this morning, Royce," she apologized, "but everyone will be there, and we'd so like to have you and Craig to come."

He thanked her and told her they would be there. He would leave the office early and drive to the park where the picnic was to be held in the little town twenty-five or thirty miles away.

He was just hanging up when a peculiar feeling came over him. It didn't sneak in through a crack in his sub-conscious. It shouldered its way into reality brazenly, forcing all else aside.

Today was the day he was going to meet the girl he would marry.

The thought stunned him.

Martha Laird misread the look on his face.

"Royce," she said, "is it bad news? Is there something wrong?"

At first he didn't even hear her. She repeated the question.

"Oh, no," he retorted lamely. "It's nothing like that. Aunt Sally wants me to bring Craig and come to their family picnic tonight, that's all."

Mrs. Laird snorted and turned back to the stove.

"That poor child ought to be home in bed," she grumbled, "instead of gallivanting around half the night. It'll be a wonder to me if he's not sick tomorrow."

Royce did not answer her. Where Craig was concerned there was no reasoning with Mrs. Laird. There were times when she acted as though the boy was hers, and Royce was just a necessary means of livelihood.

At the office he found a knotty construction problem on his desk that took all of his attention, forcing the wave of excitement and wonder aside. Not until the middle of the afternoon did he think of it again.

His first reaction was that it was one of those inexplainable tricks of the mind, a prank of his subconscious because of the aching, lonely void in his life. Soon the feeling would disappear and that would be the end of it.

Still, even if nothing came of the incident, it had been startling. As he thought about it once more the same emotion took hold of him. It was not as boisterous or demanding of attention as before. Now it was simply a calm assurance of what was about to take place, an assurance that would not be pushed aside.

As the time came for him to leave for the picnic he was as confused as ever. If it did work out the way this strange feeling indicated, it would be doubly strange to have the girl come from among Rita's relatives. Of course that didn't seem likely. He knew everyone who would be there, and he couldn't think of a girl in her family who could even be a remote possibility.

There was one thing sure, he promised himself. He wasn't going to that picnic looking for anyone, he wasn't going to make a fool of himself.

The crowd at the family gathering was about what he had expected. Relatives had come from Texas and Colorado and there was a good deal of laughter and the recalling of things that had happened years before.

With Craig in his arms Royce wandered aimlessly from one group to the other. Everyone did what they could to make him feel that he was welcome and still one of them. The women came up and made over Craig, remarking how much he looked like Rita. The men observed the boy's sturdy build and wondered if he was out for football yet. For Royce this was another tie with Rita, and he clung desperately to it. Yet, despite everyone's effort to include him, the situation wasn't the same. It would never be the same again. Only with Aunt Sally and one or two others would he be able to maintain the same relationship.

At dark the picnic broke up and Royce drove home. He left Craig with Mrs. Laird and told her he was going to the café for a cup of coffee.

"I'll be back in a little while," he called over his shoulder.

She was growling in an undertone about needing her sleep and being awakened in the middle of the night as he went down the steps. But by this time he was used to her complaining. He paid no attention to it as he got into his car and drove down to a small café on the edge of the business district.

Joe Christy, who had just gone on the Glenville police force, was in the café when he entered.

"Hi, Royce, come over and sit down."

Royce saw that his friend was not in uniform. "I thought they were going to get wise to you, but I didn't think it would happen this soon."

Joe laughed.

"There's where you're wrong. I've been able to fool them so far."

They were still talking when the café door opened and two girls came in. Royce didn't even notice them until his companion punched him significantly with his forefinger.

"There she is," he said in an undertone. "There's Linda, the girl I was telling you about."

Slowly Royce set his coffee cup on the counter and turned on the stool to glance in the direction Joe indicated. The girls had stopped just inside the door and were looking for a booth. They were so near the same size they could have been twins, short, slender and smartly dressed. But there the similarity ended. One was dark-haired and of olive complexion to match the brown of her eyes. She was not exactly a pretty girl, Royce noted. Her features were too sharp to suit him and her mouth too large. Yet there was a certain attractiveness about her.

Royce was still studying her obliquely when she saw Joe. Her face seemed to come alive and she waved to him, a quick, dignified little wave. Grinning self-consciously, Joe slid off the stool and approached her.

Royce turned his attention to Linda's blonde companion. He had never seen her before that he could recall. She was as fair as Linda was dark. Her soft blonde hair was cut short and crowned with a perky blue hat that brought out the color of her eyes and was as jaunty and gay as her smile.

He didn't know whether she was beautiful or not. All he was sure about was that when she smiled her entire being seemed to come alive, and even from a distance he could see the pixie-like gleam in her eyes. She would be, he decided as he looked at her, an interesting person to get to know.

However, he was not prepared to get to know her that evening. He was tired after the picnic and was much more interested in getting home and getting to bed than in meeting anyone. As Joe started in his direction, the two girls in tow, Royce got off the stool quickly and in desperation glanced at the door. Had they not been between him and the only exit he would have whirled and hurried away.

"Royce," Joe said, "I'd like to have you meet Linda Morris and Penny Turner."

Linda's smile was warm and friendly, but reserved. It was obvious that she wasn't looking for a pickup any more than he was. Yet she was gracious and well mannered. He liked that. He was always suspicious of girls who threw themselves at a fellow. Not that it had ever happened to him; he wasn't the kind they went crazy over.

Before he realized what was happening, he was sitting in a booth beside Penny, and Joe and Linda were on the other side. At first he tried to excuse himself.

"I'd better be getting home," he said. "If I come in late I'm afraid I'll waken Craig or, worse yet, Mrs. Laird. Craig's my little boy, you know."

He didn't know why he had to blurt out that information at that particular time. It didn't seem necessary at all.

"Craig is Royce's son," Joe explained quickly before the anger could flash in Penny's eyes at being tricked into sitting in a café booth with a married man. "His wife died when the baby was born, and Mrs. Laird is keeping house for him."

"And what a housekeeper she is," Royce added. "She rules both Craig and me."

Joe assumed they would be taking the girls home. He picked up the check, paid it, and guided Linda toward the door.

"Where's your car, Royce?" he asked, leaving his friend no alternative except to follow with Penny.

Royce felt uneasy as he backed away from the curb with Penny at his side. What if someone had seen him with her?

"That's just like a stepmother! I'll go to Auntie," was Barry's escape from restrictions and responsibilities.

Photo story is taken from the film *My Son, My Son*, used by courtesy of Ken Anderson Films, Winona Lake, Indiana. The names used for the characters in the book are not the same as the names used in the film.

Barry went off to college, and returned a seemingly normal young man ready for the responsibilities of an adult.

He married Kathryn, and they began life together happily enough.

Unknown to his parents, Barry had developed a new habit—and the local tavern provided the opportunity.

"We need food" was no longer a strong enough plea to hand over a paycheck.

Horses and winning
in rodeos became
Barry's obsessions.

His work in the family monument business suffered.

Not even the ignominy of being jailed as a drunk changed Barry's ways.

Bernie and Marge thought they had done their best, but they saw no results until they let go and let God.

In a church prayer meeting, Bernie publicly admitted defeat and the need for prayer.

Barry finally accepted Christ as his Saviour just weeks before his death. God had acted!

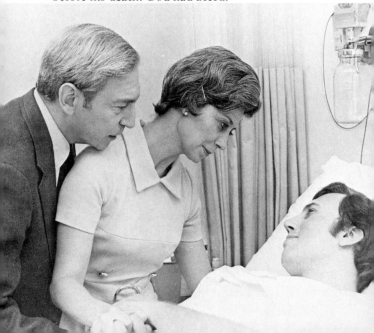

he wondered. What would they think? What sort of stories would get started around that grubby, gossipy little town? He had no right to be out with anyone, even for a casual ride that wasn't of his doing. Hadn't he loved Rita? Didn't her memory mean anything to him?

He glanced at the girl beside him. There was no denying that she was attractive, or that he found her interesting.

For a time he drove in silence, buffeted by the conflicting emotions that surged and ebbed within him. At last, slowly, he became aware that Penny was studying his somber face, a smile lighting her delicate features.

"What should we talk about?" she asked. "The weather? That's always a nice, safe subject."

A crooked grin tugged at the corners of his mouth.

"We ought to be able to find something more interesting than that," he told her, "if we try hard."

"What about that little boy of yours?" she asked, interest glittering in her eyes. "I've always been partial to little boys."

He hadn't intended saying anything more about Craig than he had already told her but, surprisingly, she acted as though she really wanted to hear about him. She asked how big he was and what he weighed and how many words he could say. She wanted to know about the color of his eyes and hair and if he looked like him. Royce found himself describing Craig in detail, telling her some of the funny little things he had done and how he seemed to live for the times when his daddy came home to play with him.

"I suppose he misses his mother without realizing it," she said.

He shot a quick, questioning look in her direction. She seemed to understand how it was with Craig. He couldn't help asking about it.

Her smile flashed.

"I know what it's like," she said softly. "I lost my daddy when I was eight years old."

The corners of Royce's mouth straightened. Somehow he had never considered the fact that others had gone through turmoil. She would probably understand about Rita too. He found himself telling her all about his wife, how happy they had been together and of the grief that all but crushed him when she died.

It was the first time in months that he had been able to talk at length with anyone about Rita. She listened attentively to what he was saying, the same as Aunt Sally had done, and asked him about his late wife in such a way that he felt free to continue. She was so open, so natural in her attitude.

Talking with her was so different than talking with some of his oldest and closest friends. Those who knew Rita best usually squirmed uncomfortably if he chanced to mention her, and changed the subject as soon as possible. Strange how freely he could talk to this slight, attractive young stranger. Before he had known her an hour it seemed that a bond had been forged between them.

4

PENNY, IN TURN, told Royce about herself and her family. She had only been eight years old at the time, but she still remembered the horror on her mother's ashen face as she came home from school that winter afternoon.

She came bursting into the house, arms loaded with books that she hadn't had to bring home. It had been a wonderful day. The teacher gave her a hundred in spelling for the third time that week and she got to play with Sue Hanscomb and Millie Elwood at recess. And she thought she might get the part of the good fairy in the operetta their school was going to give.

There were so many good things to tell that she had run all the way home. She hadn't even stopped to throw snowballs at Stevie Baxter when he threw one at her.

"Mother!" she cried, dashing through the door. "Mother!"

Her mother was in the bedroom. Even though she hadn't answered, Penny could hear her.

"Mother!" She opened the door, blue eyes rounding as she saw that her mother was putting on her best dress. That was something she seldom did unless she was going to the women's meeting at church. "Are you going someplace?"

Then she saw the tears in her mother's eyes. Her own joy died on her happy young face.

"What's the matter?"

Her older sister took her by the arm and drew her away.

"We've got to go over and stay with Grandma tonight," she whispered. "Daddy is awful sick and they had to take him to the hospital."

Dimly Penny understood about hospitals. She knew that was where mothers went to get their babies, and some of her friends at school had been in the hospital for a day or so when they had their tonsils out. But she couldn't understand about her daddy being sick.

He was the strongest man in the whole world. He was the one who swung her so high on their backyard swing that her stomach did flip-flops, and if he hadn't been with her it would have been no fun at all. He was the one who held her in his arms when she didn't feel good from eating too much watermelon or ice cream, and who kissed her tears away and fixed her broken wagon.

He couldn't be sick. Not Daddy! He was too strong and too wonderful to be sick. There had to be some mistake.

Nobody talked much over at Grandma's that night. Nobody even told her when it was time to go to bed and Grandpa wouldn't tell her a story. He didn't say and she didn't think she should ask him why he couldn't, but she was sure it had something to do with her daddy being in the hospital.

She remembered kneeling impulsively by the bed before getting in with her older sister, Elna.

"God bless Daddy and make him well real soon so he can come home from the hospital," she prayed.

Grandma started to cry a little and went into the other room. Penny was afraid she had done something wrong, but Mother had always told them to ask God about things like that and she did *want* Daddy out of the hospital.

Sometime during the night her mother came home. When Penny got up the next morning everyone else was up and dressed. Grandpa called her over to him and put his arm about her tenderly.

"You won't be going to school this morning, Penny," he said. And then he told her that her daddy had gone to heaven, that God wanted him there to help Him.

Penny hadn't cried. How could she cry when she could not even understand what had happened?

The days that followed were blurred and jumbled until she could not separate them, even yet. She must have gone to the funeral, but she did not remember much about it. All she knew for sure was that she spent a lot more time at Grandma and Grandpa's than she had ever spent before. And nobody laughed much around their house anymore.

Other things were different too. Her oldest brother, Sid, quit school and started working in a service station. Penny hadn't understood why at first. Mother hadn't wanted him to and cried a lot about it when he told her what he had done.

"But I've got to, Mom," he protested. "Somebody has to take care of you and the other kids, and I'm the oldest."

Her other brother got a job in a local store stocking shelves after school and on Saturday, and Elna did baby-sitting. Their mother also got a job doing housework two days a week for the banker up the street. The whole family worked, except Penny.

This didn't seem to register with her either, except that nobody was home much anymore.

She found, however, that not having a father made differences in other ways as well.

The kids in her grade had been talking about the picnic for weeks. It was the last event before school let out for the summer and they were going down to the park and have pop and ice cream and everything. They used to have those things at home quite often, but since Daddy died they hadn't had either. But now they were going to have the picnic and everybody in her grade would be there. She was so excited she ran all the way home to tell her mother about it.

"And I've got to have fifteen cents by Monday," she concluded breathlessly, "so Miss Peterson will have time to buy the refreshments."

Her mother looked up wearily but did not answer.

"We don't have to take the money until Monday, but Mary is taking hers in the morning so she'll be sure and not forget it. I told her I'd do that too." She paused, eyeing her mother hopefully. "Can I, Mother? Can I?"

"I'll talk it over with Sid when he gets home tonight."

Penny's lower lip quivered.

"Mary's mother doesn't have to talk it over with anybody," she replied. "She just gives her the fifteen cents whenever she wants it."

"I know." Her mother kissed her on the cheek.

The following morning, instead of the money Miss Peterson asked her to bring, Penny's mother gave her a note to take to the teacher. It was in a tightly sealed envelope with Miss Peterson's name written on the outside.

Penny looked at it, disappointment clouding her pretty young face.

"We weren't supposed to bring notes from our mothers," she protested. "We're supposed to bring fifteen cents."

"Give that to Miss Peterson," her mother ordered with a sternness she usually reserved for the times when she and Elna or the boys were fighting.

That morning the distance to school was the longest Penny had ever known it to be. All the other kids in her grade would be bringing their fifteen cents, but she had to bring a note. At first she felt as though she couldn't go on to school that day, that she would sneak down into the park and hide so nobody could find her. She'd tear that note in little pieces and throw it away, and when her mother asked about it she'd tell her that Miss Peterson threw the note in the wastepaper basket without reading it.

But she knew she couldn't do that. She always minded her mother. At least she tried to mind her. She couldn't deliberately do something like staying away from school when she knew that she was supposed to go every day.

Miss Peterson read the note over twice and went to the

principal's office holding it in her hand. Penny saw what had taken place and squirmed uneasily. She couldn't imagine what was going to take place, but it must not be good or Miss Peterson wouldn't be going to the principal's office.

Maybe they were mad at her about the note and weren't going to let her go to the picnic at all now. That was probably it. Miss Peterson had gotten angry and was going to tell the principal that she didn't want Penny at the picnic. If that happened, she reasoned, she wasn't going to go to school that day.

She'd get sick first. She'd eat Grandpa's crab apples until she got the stomachache. That's what she'd do. Then everybody would be sorry.

Only Grandpa didn't have any crab apples yet. He wouldn't have any all summer until just before school started in the fall. So she'd have to think of something else—something like holding her breath until her face turned purple. Then nobody would know what was the matter with her and they would probably call the doctor and have to send her home in an ambulance. Then her mother would be sorry she hadn't given her the money. Everybody at school would be sorry.

She was still enjoying thinking of all the terrible things that would happen to her when she held her breath the day of the picnic when Miss Peterson came back into the room. And, sure enough! She came directly to Penny's desk. The girl's gaze came up miserably.

Penny?"

"Y-Yes."

"Tell your mother it will be all right."

Penny stared at her questioningly.

"She'll understand," Miss Peterson said mysteriously.

When Penny brought home the strange message her mother nodded.

"I thought it would be. I wrapped it for you this morning."

The girl's eyes rounded curiously.

"Didn't I tell you?" her mother asked. "I wrote Miss Peterson that we wouldn't be able to pay the fifteen cents for

39

your class picnic but that I would send a jar of pickles that I canned last fall."

Pickles! She had to take pickles to the picnic! Penny died a thousand deaths.

But she couldn't say anything that would let her mother know how she felt about taking a jar of pickles for the picnic instead of money like the other kids brought. Instinctively she knew how hard it was for her mother those days. She wasn't going to do anything that would make it worse.

She took the pickles with her that noon, walking the long way to school so she wouldn't meet any of her friends on the way, and sneaking them into the principal's office when she thought no one was looking.

After that it became standard practice for her to bring pickles or a jar of canned fruit when there was a picnic at school. She grew to hate those occasions.

Penny didn't know how Sid and the older kids felt about their mother getting married again, but she was pleased about it herself. It meant that Mother would be able to stay home, for one thing, instead of going out to work, and, for another, Penny missed her dad so very much. It wasn't the same as having her own daddy, but her mother's new husband was a good man and seemed to love all of them as much as his own four children. She found it easy to call him "Dad."

When she was in the seventh grade the boys began to notice her soft blonde hair and quick smile. She accepted their attention casually, as though it was her due, much to the annoyance of some of the other girls who found the boys they liked enamored with Penny.

The pudgy, freckled-faced boy who sat at the desk in front of her painstakingly printed his message on his thumbnail: "If you love me, smile," and held it back for her to see.

Others argued bitterly over the privilege of carrying her books home from school. She had the usual crushes during her years in school, falling hard for the usual number of awkward, pimply boys, but she was as changeable as the wind, and just as frivolous. Elna, who was working her way through college by this time, was horrified at Penny's lack of stability.

"Mother," she would say, "you've got to do something about Penny."

Mother would look at her oldest daughter and smile indulgently. Penny had an idea that her mother fully intended to talk to her about it, but never did get around to it. Her mother was like that, carefully avoiding anything that was unpleasant.

Elna talked with Penny a number of times herself. She listened politely, but that was all. She didn't see why it was so bad going with half a dozen boys at the same time. In fact, it was sort of fun.

She didn't tell Royce about that, however. Nor did she tell him she already had a special boyfriend, even now. She didn't think that would interest him. She went on to tell him how Sid had gone on to Bible school after being relieved of the responsibility for supporting the family, and Elna and their other brother had gone to college.

"Dad Benson has been as good to me as my own father," she concluded at last, "but money has been so scarce I haven't felt that I could go on to college without working for a couple of years first."

"Things haven't been easy for you either," Royce acknowledged.

The smile faded from her face, but returned as quickly as it left.

"No," she admitted, "but I can't complain either. I've been having too much fun."

He looked her way again, eyes narrowing. That was a peculiar thing to say.

Presently the boys stopped in front of the house where Linda and Penny had an apartment, and took them to the door.

"Thank you so much," Penny said, smiling. "It's been a delightful evening."

She and Linda stood just inside the door until the car pulled away.

"He's the most interesting fellow I've ever been with," Penny murmured.

"I thought you were supposed to be going steady."

A strange look gleamed in Penny's eyes.

"As a matter of fact, so did I."

Royce drove thoughtfully home that night after letting Joe Christy out. He was just making the discovery that he had enjoyed himself more during that brief interlude than he had at any time for months. It was not until he was in bed, however, that he remembered the unusual feeling that had persisted all day, the feeling that he was going to meet his future wife before the day was out.

Penny had been pleasant to be around, he had to admit, but she was probably only twenty or twenty-one and looked younger than that by several years. A personality girl like her would have a string of boyfriends and wouldn't be wanting to date a fellow who had a three-year-old son. It was probably just a coincidence that he had met her that night. Nothing would ever come of it. Royce pushed thoughts of Penny aside and promptly went to sleep.

He had no intention of ever seeing her again. Indeed, for a week, he didn't think of her at all. Then he was driving home from work one evening when he caught sight of Penny, arms loaded with groceries, walking the same direction he was going. Impulsively he pulled over to the side of the street and stopped near her.

"Taxi?"

"Oh, hello," she smiled, approaching the car. "You're a knight in shining armor. I was beginning to think I was going to collapse on the street before I got home."

He took the sacks from her and put them in the back seat.

"I'm truly grateful, Royce," she said seriously. "I was getting awfully tired."

Before she got out he had asked her to go to dinner with him the following evening. Surprisingly, she accepted. After that he was with her regularly, enjoying himself more with each succeeding date.

After the second or third time they were together she insisted that he bring Craig along the next time he came to see her.

"He's been after me to take him out to the fair and let him ride the merry-go-round," he said. "We could do that tomorrow night if you'd like."

Her eyes sparkled.

"It's a date," she exclaimed. "That is, if I can ride the merry-go-round too."

That was one of the things he liked about her. She was gay and happy and completely unpredictable.

Craig took instinctively to Penny from the first moment he saw her, as though she was someone special in both his and his dad's lives. He wanted to sit on her lap in the car and kept asking her to help him put on his sweater or take it off—anything to get her to do something for him. When he tired of that, he took her purse and, balancing it on his fat little knees, clasped it tightly with both hands.

"I've got your purse now," he informed her. "You're not going to be able to leave Daddy and me."

At the noisy fairground he reached chubby fingers up to take her hand.

"I like you," he murmured.

"I like you too," she replied, squeezing his hand reassuringly.

After that Craig plagued Royce to take him along when he went to see Penny which, at this time, was at least twice a week.

"I want to go with you, Daddy," he would plead. "I want to see Penny too."

Martha Laird snorted her indignation but voiced no other protest.

Before another six months had passed, Royce and Penny were engaged and had set the date for their wedding. Rita's Aunt Sally heard about it and came to the office to talk to him.

"I hope you won't think I'm interfering, Royce," she said,

her voice taut with emotion. "But I had to talk with you. I'm concerned about Craig."

He eyed her narrowly, but remained silent.

"I know you love him, Royce, and have given him a good home. But now—" Her lips trembled. "I just want you to know that we—we'll be only too happy to have Craig come and live with us if that will be better for him and for you and Penny."

Had it been anyone else Royce might have been angry, thinking it was nothing one way or the other to anyone else whether he and Penny married or what they did about Craig. But nobody got angry with Aunt Sally. Least of all him. He could not doubt her motives, the earnestness of her manner. And she was so careful of what she said so she would not be misunderstood.

As gently as possible Royce talked wtih Aunt Sally about Penny. He tried to tell her what sort of person she was and how genuinely she loved Craig.

"And, actually, Aunt Sally," he said, "Craig seems to love Penny every bit as much as she loves him. When she's around he won't let anyone else do anything for him."

"I'm glad to hear that." There was a trace of doubt in her voice.

"This is something I've been terribly concerned about," he continued. "If I wasn't sure in my own mind that Penny will treat Craig just as she would treat a child of her own, I'd call it all off right now."

Aunt Sally's gaze met his.

"I hope so," she said softly. "I sincerely hope she treats him the way he should be treated. It would break my heart if he wasn't."

The week before the wedding Royce told Mrs. Laird that they would not be needing her services any longer. She did not seem to be surprised. If she hadn't heard of the approaching marriage she would surely have guessed it from the amount of time Royce and Penny were spending together.

She took the news without comment.

"We'll be going on a short honeymoon," he continued,

"and would like to have you keep Craig while we're gone, but it's our plan to be back by the first."

"I see." Her lips clamped tightly on the words.

When they returned she had already moved most of her things out and had her suitcase packed to take with her.

"I hope you'll be good to Craig, Mrs. Lawson," she said, her voice choking.

Craig looked up at her curiously.

"Why does Mrs. Laird have to move?" he asked. His lower jaw trembled. "Can't she stay too?"

Penny knelt beside the boy, her slim young arm about his shoulder affectionately.

"Mrs. Laird is only going to be moving up the street a block," she told him. "You can go up and visit with her whenever you want to."

The boy looked from Penny to Mrs. Laird and over to his dad in bewilderment.

"But why does she have to leave?"

5

CRAIG SOON FORGOT his disappointment that Martha Laird had to move out in his joy that Penny would be taking care of him. Those first few days he could do nothing for himself. She had to help him pull on his shoes, button his shirt, and get his coat out of the closet. At the table he crowded his chair as close to hers as possible, insisting that she butter his bread and help him cut his meat.

"We're getting sort of helpless all of a sudden, aren't we, Craig?" Royce would ask, teasing. "What's the deal?"

His son eyed him narrowly but did not answer him. He knew what his dad was talking about, but he pretended not to.

"Now, Daddy," Penny would defend him. "If Craig wants me to help him, that's just between the two of us, isn't it, Craig? You don't have to concern yourself about it."

The boy's face brightened and he flashed Penny a very special grin.

"Well, I guess it's all right," Royce replied, trying to sound stern and unhappy, "if that's the way it's got to be. But I sure don't get much attention."

She wrinkled her nose at him.

Royce wished Aunt Sally could see Penny and Craig together this way. She would no longer be concerned about his son and wondering about whether or not he was going to be loved.

At night when it was time for Craig to go to bed there was a certain ritual he followed. He would gather up all of his books for Penny to read to him, a chore that had formerly been reserved for Royce. Even Martha Laird had been unable to read to him. When the last of the books was finished Craig would squirm about on her lap so he could plead with his eyes.

"Now tell me a story."

"It's getting late, Craig," she told him. "You should have been asleep ages ago."

"Please, tell me a story. Just a short one."

"About this long?" She measured a space with her thumb and forefinger. Her voice was serious, but her eyes danced merrily.

"Longer than that. About this long." He stretched his short arms to their very limit.

"All right." She was laughing by this time. "But I'll only tell you one story. Then it's off to bed. OK?"

"OK," he promised.

He was not above trying to coax for another story if he thought he could wangle her into it, but he usually knew when she could no longer be induced to entertain him and provide an excuse for him to stay up past his bedtime.

Then she had to go into his bedroom with him, listen to his brief prayer, and tuck the blanket about his sturdy young form. Once in a while Penny would pretend she wasn't going to kiss him good night. It was only a game of pretend and Craig entered into it heartily. He captured her about the neck with his fat little hands and held her firmly, eyes dancing.

"You forgot something," he would remind her the way she would remind his dad if he started to work without kissing her and Craig good-bye.

"So I did." She used Royce's words and his boyish inflection. Craig giggled with delight as she put her arms about him and held him close to her.

47

On one such occasion a couple of weeks or so after they returned home from their honeymoon, he still clung to her after the good-night kiss.

"Know what?" he asked.

She shook her head.

"Try to guess."

She wrinkled her forehead as though she was thinking as hard as she could.

"I give up."

"I'm not going to call you Aunt Penny, anymore. I'm going to call you 'Mother.' That's what Eddie calls his mom."

Penny grabbed him close to keep him from seeing the tears in her eyes. She and Royce had talked that over before they were married and had decided they would wait until Craig was well adjusted to her before getting him to call her "mother." Now he had taken the matter out of their hands and chose to call her "mother" on his own. She couldn't help crying.

*   *   *

A change had taken place in Royce's life since Rita's death. When they were first married they started going to her church and attended regularly. In Glenville church attendance was the accepted thing and much of the community life revolved around the church. It was good for business and a help socially.

Rita had been much more serious about church attendance than Royce had been. She was born into the church and was baptized, and at the age of twelve or thirteen she attended the instruction class and became a member.

Royce became a church member too after they were married, and set up an office in her hometown. Church hadn't meant enough to him even to suggest that they attend the denomination his folks belonged to. Actually, he had never thought much about religion one way or the other. It was all right, he guessed. His folks seemed to get a lot out of going, but he had gotten out of the habit when he took a Sunday job at a service station while he was still in high school and hadn't gone to church more than half a dozen times during his college years. It wasn't that he was opposed to it. It just didn't mean anything to him.

When Royce and Rita were married one of the first things she asked him about was going to church with her. So he did. His ideas about religion didn't change any, but her church meant so much to her that he knew it pleased her to have him go with her. And he did have to admit that he enjoyed the parties their Sunday school class held. Even more, he enjoyed the work various church members turned his way.

It made him think of a lecturer at one of the first meetings of architects he attended a few months after graduation.

"Those of you who aren't active in a church are missing the best source of contacts in your community. You never know when the man sitting in the pew next to you or serving with you on the board will be planning a new building. Your contact with him in church can very well be the deciding factor in your getting the job."

Before Rita's death Royce would have agreed with him, had he been completely honest with himself. But that wasn't all. He would also have said that business reasons would have been the most important aspect of belonging to a church.

Her death, however, was a shattering experience and bombarded his consciousness with dozens of questions he could not answer. What was the meaning of life? Was it just to be born, live a span and die? Was that the total of existence? Was there no more to living than the years on this troubled earth? Did Rita still live? Would he ever see her again? Or did she lie in the grave?

He had been in the cemetery examining the small monument he placed at his wife's grave when all the questions seemed to roll into one and hit him forcibly. Was that piece of granite more durable and lasting than either he or Rita?

He tried to think back to what he had been taught in philosophy classes at college. The philosophers they studied had pleasing words and soothing, high-sounding phrases that he thought at the time had the answers to every situation.

49

God is the Father and all mankind are His children and brothers, one with another. There is a little of God in each of us. He is the embodiment of love. Only in loving can men enjoy life's richest experience. Loving and serving others gives meaning to what men do.

There was truth in what they had to say, he reasoned. Theirs was the intelligent, intellectual approach to life and its meaning. After all, they represented man's finest, most penetrating independent thought. They had to be true.

But that had been before he looked death in the face and saw it in all its horror—in its dread finality.

When life ceased, what then? The philosophers tried for answers, but in his need they stood empty and meaningless, as helpless as the doctor who tried to keep Rita's life from ebbing.

Royce went back to those books he had studied so avidly in college, thinking perhaps that he had not seen the importance of resolving such problems and had missed their solutions. But there was nothing he could find that satisfied in their views of death; nothing that could give strength and comfort to an aching heart.

Turning to the Bible had not occurred to Royce, although he sought out the thinking of philosophers, but he did go to the minister of the church he and Rita had been attending.

"The church teaches that there is a life after death," Rev. Barker said in answer to his embarrassed, stammering question. "But life with God eternally isn't the right of every man. Eternal life is only for those who have met His conditions."

He went on to talk about Jesus Christ who had a claim on the heart and life of each person, and how every man was going to have to give account to God of what he had personally done with Christ. Had he confessed he was wicked and unprofitable and put his trust in the Lord Jesus Christ to save him? Or had he turned his back on Christ and walked in his own way?

Royce asked few questions and the elderly, graying minister did not press him, but told him to think seriously about what he had told him.

"I'll be praying for you," he promised when he said goodbye at his study door.

He didn't know why, but Barker's simple statement irritated him at the time. It was not until months later that he was able to appreciate the older man's concern.

Talking with Rev. Barker made Royce think of that afternoon years before when he had gone with his folks to special meetings in the City Auditorium back home. As he recalled, he must have been ten or eleven at the time. They had been going as a family all week and he was tired of sitting still and listening to sermons. He and a few other kids were sitting in the balcony at the back trying to listen as little as possible. But at the close of the service when the invitation was given for all of those who wanted to follow Christ to hold up their hands, he was one of the first.

He went down to the inquiry room in the basement as the evangelist asked those who had held up their hands to do, and wandered around, not knowing what was going to happen next. There had been quite a number of people there talking by twos in low tones or kneeling among the chairs in prayer. He waited for someone to come up to him, but nobody did. After a time he went out and promptly forgot the incident. He didn't know why it had come to mind at this particular time.

Maybe Rev. Barker and the evangelist back home were talking about the same thing. Although the matter was still unresolved as far as his thinking was concerned, he did know that he had a different outlook on many things after his wife's death.

"Life's too short to spend it fighting with each other," he told Penny on one occasion shortly after they were married. "We never know how long we're going to live. Why spoil it by quarreling?"

She nodded her agreement. She had never thought of it in quite that way, but she knew she would never want to argue with this shy, quiet man she had married.

51

"Another thing," he continued. "We're going to enjoy life day by day and not be so ambitious and covetous we've got to break our necks trying to get ahead, or to get something nicer than somebody else has."

She smiled contentedly and leaned back in his arms.

"It's always going to be like this, isn't it, Royce?" she asked.

He bent and kissed her, trying not to remember that the dread specter of death could separate them, even as it had separated him and Rita. He wasn't going to quarrel with her the way he and Rita had quarreled during those difficult first months of adjustment. He wasn't going to have memory pull and tear at him because of the cruel, angered things he had said. He didn't know whether he could keep Penny as happy as she was at this moment, but he did know that he was going to try.

At first Craig was so enraptured with Penny and having her live with them that he didn't think of going over to see Martha Laird. He might never have thought of seeing her again had she not lived so close he met her on the sidewalk in front of the house one afternoon.

"You don't ever come and see me, Craig," she told him, reproach in her voice.

He looked up sheepishly.

"I've been so lonesome for you."

"I'll come and see you tomorrow," he said.

"Promise?"

"If Mother will let me."

"I'll bake some cookies if you'll come."

His eyes danced. "Chocolate chip?"

"Chocolate chip."

After that he went to see her two or three times a week. When he decided it was time for a visit, he would open the screen with a grubby hand and call out to Penny, "I'm going over to see Aunt Martha, Mother." Then, fat knees pumping, he ran the length of the block to Martha Laird's apartment in the big house on the corner.

6

It was not long until Rev. Barker took a church on the West Coast and a younger man took his place. James Crandall was about Royce's age, an energetic young minister not long out of seminary. His class had voted him the student most likely to succeed, and he was determined to make that prediction come true at the earliest possible moment. He had plans for getting every department in the church functioning at top efficiency, and the ability to work with people. Everybody loved him.

About the same time a minister friend of Penny's came back to town to hold special meetings in his former church. The Sunday they were to begin she mentioned him to Royce.

"You remember hearing me talk about Rev. Arland Mills, don't you?" she asked.

"You stayed with his family and went to high school, didn't you?"

"I didn't think you remembered."

"I remember a lot of things about you."

"I stayed with them for a year or two after Daddy and Mother were married and moved out on the farm."

"And I suppose you'd like to go and hear him," Royce said.

"Actually, I want to go so I can talk to him for a few minutes afterward. He and his wife were so nice to me."

Their own church didn't have evening services, and Royce couldn't remember having gone to church on Sunday night since he was a kid back home, but he agreed to go with Penny that night to hear her old friend. After all, he told himself, the Mills family had meant a great deal in her life. He could understand why she would want to go and see him again.

Royce was completely captured by the massive minister. There was such force—such conviction in his voice. Here was no cultured, well-trained oratory, no high-sounding phrases as he bent over the pulpit and flayed the air with a hamlike fist. The speaker may have been well educated; Royce supposed he was. But it wasn't education speaking; it was a man thundering from the depths of great convictions.

That was the thing that first gripped Royce. Here was an individual who believed what he was saying. He didn't have to dip into the murky mélange of philosophy in the vain hope that he could somehow come up with something that would satisfy the longing of his heart. He knew what he believed.

That, in itself, was enough to draw Royce to him.

He had never heard anyone quote the Bible as much as this man did, or accord it the position of authority.

"I am the door: by me if any man enter in, he shall be saved, and shall go in and out, and find pasture."*

Royce slid forward in the pew, unmindful of his small son or his wife beside him. In that moment he was unmindful of anyone else in that large sanctuary except himself and the speaker.

All that Rev. Barker had said to Royce became clear as Mills continued to speak. God is a holy God and cannot tolerate sin. He provided the law for man, but man was so weak, so self-willed, so determined to do evil that he hadn't been able to live up to the law. But God had provided a way
*John 10:9.

54

for man to escape the just punishment for his sin by sending His Son to live a sinless life and die on the cross so that all men could be saved.

It was all there in the story of the shepherd and the sheep. Jesus is the door. If a man wants to go to heaven, he has to go through the door. He has to meet the conditions God set down by sending Jesus Christ to give His life on the cross. And if a person met those conditions he would become one of Jesus' flock and could go in and out and find pasture.

It was strange but he had never understood that before, even in all the times he had gone to church and listened to Rev. Barker and the new minister who took his place. Now the curtain had been drawn aside and he could understand all that had been said before.

The following night he suggested that they go to church again. Penny could not contain her surprise.

"I like that guy," he told her. "He believes what he preaches."

They went almost every night for the entire two weeks. Royce could never remember a similar period with as much meaning for him. He saw that some of the people sitting around them carried Bibles to church and looked up the references as the speaker went along. He had never taken his Bible to church before, but it seemed a good idea to him. The next night he had Penny dig out one of their Bibles so he could take it to services. After that he had it with him every night, looking up reference after reference. The only problem was that he began reading and, if he wasn't careful, he would forget to listen to the minister.

It was with real reluctance that Royce saw the series of meetings end. There was so much he wanted to learn—so many things he wanted to hear the speaker explain. They went to their own church Sunday morning, but on Sunday night he suggested they go to the Community Church where they had heard Mills speak.

"We ought to be going to church tonight, Penny," he said.

55

It soon became the accepted thing for them to attend the evening services at the other church.

* * *

The week before Craig's fifth birthday he began to talk about going over to Aunt Martha's for a party.

"She says nobody else is going to be invited," he told them. "She's going to bake me a cake and have ice cream and everything."

Royce's eyes twinkled.

"If Aunt Martha is having a party for you, maybe Mother and I can forget the party we've been planning to have for you."

Craig's lower lip drooped, and for a moment he looked as though he was about to cry. "But, Daddy," he protested, "Aunt Martha's is just going to be a *little* party."

Penny kissed him lovingly on the cheek.

"Don't you worry, Craig. I won't let Daddy cancel our party just because Aunt Martha is having one for you. That's a promise."

He smiled at her with trembling lips.

Usually Craig was a late sleeper, but on the morning of his birthday he was the first one out of bed. He scrambled noisily into their bedroom and tugged impatiently on the covers.

"Come on," he exclaimed. "Let's get up and have breakfast."

Penny pulled herself upright in bed and rubbed her drowsy eyes..

"So early?"

"I've got to go over to Aunt Martha's," he informed her. "Don't you remember?"

There was excitement around the house that morning, excitement that followed a prescribed ritual on birthdays. Royce chased Craig until he caught him and made a great show of swatting him five times.

"And one to grow on!"

The blows were landed with much fanfare and noise, and Craig howled in protest. That was all part of the game.

When Royce finished, the five-year-old looked up at Penny, grinning expectantly.

"And now it's my turn," she exclaimed.

That was what he was waiting for. He wriggled free of Royce's grasp and ran squealing through the house. Penny caught him in the living room.

"You needn't think you're going to get away from me on your birthday," she retorted, bending him over her knee. "Now you're going to get it good."

When she finished he looked up at her.

"Mother," he announced solemnly, "you're getting fat." As though the thought had just occurred to him, he looked her over again, an appraising gleam in his eye. "You're getting awful fat."

Royce looked at her and grinned.

"We'll tell you all about it one of these days," Penny told him.

That seemed to sate his curiosity. He turned his attention to Royce.

"Now the birthday spankings are over, Daddy. Where are my presents?"

"Presents?" Royce's eyebrows arched as though he didn't know what his son was talking about. "What presents? Am I supposed to know something about some presents?"

Craig was indignant. "When a guy has a birthday he always gets presents."

"Oh?" Royce glanced at Penny. "Did you know that, Mother? Are there supposed to be presents when a boy has a birthday?"

Craig eyed her hopefully. He thought his dad was only teasing, but he couldn't be sure. That look on his face was serious.

"It seems to me that I have heard something about birthday presents," Penny added. "Especially for boys who are five years old."

Triumph gleamed in Craig's face.

"Where are they, Dad?" he insisted.

"We'll see if there are any presents for you at your birthday party tonight. OK?"

He went over to Martha Laird's shortly before noon, pulling his coaster wagon.

"Well," Penny said, meeting him at the door. "I was beginning to think you were going to stay all day." There was light-hearted banter in her voice.

"Aunt Martha had the bestest party," he exclaimed, excitement still sparkling in his soft blue eyes. "She had ice cream and cake and everything!"

He was trying to get something out of his wagon as he talked. Penny went out to help him.

"And what have you got there?"

"She made this cake for me."

"How nice."

Craig's sturdy figure stiffened slightly. "Aunt Martha said I was supposed to eat it all by myself."

Penny frowned. That wasn't the way they wanted to raise Craig. They wanted him to be warm and openhearted, not possessive and selfish. But it was his birthday. Perhaps that was what Martha was thinking.

"Well, I know it's your birthday," she told him, "but you know how well Daddy likes cake. Don't you think it would be all right just to give him a little piece."

Craig's somber gaze went down to the cake and then up at her.

"Well," he replied with considerable reluctance, "I suppose I could give Daddy a little piece."

Penny helped him carry his cake and the presents Mrs. Laird bought for him into the house. There was an unusual possessiveness in his manner as he gathered up the gifts and took them into his room—a possessiveness Penny had never seen in him before. He wanted to have his cake in his room on the dresser so no one else would be getting into it.

"I think we had better leave it in the kitchen," Penny told him.

"But it's mine. Aunt Martha gave it to me."

"I know it's yours, but food belongs in the kitchen. That's where we'll keep your cake."

He studied her reproachfully, as though he could no longer trust her.

Penny was greatly troubled by Craig's new attitude toward her. It was almost as though something had come between them that day, something to spoil the warm, happy relationship they had enjoyed. But it wasn't long until he was himself again. And when the time came for him to take his nap he wanted her to read to him. As she did so her concern ebbed away.

Royce came home from the office a bit earlier than usual that night, his arms loaded with mysterious packages. Craig met him at the door, eyes shining.

"What have you got, Daddy?"

"Never you mind what I've got." There was mock irritation in his voice.

His son looked up at him. "What have you got, Daddy?" he repeated.

"What makes you think these packages concern you?"

"I know they do. Today's my birthday."

"And maybe you're mistaken about these packages belonging to you," his dad told him. "Did you ever think of that?"

Craig stopped teasing. He hadn't really wanted to know what was in the packages, that would spoil everything. He wanted them all wrapped pretty and brought out at the proper time. They would have dinner first and then the cake and ice cream. Then they would sing "Happy Birthday" to him and Mother would have Daddy get the packages. That was the way it was the most fun.

In spite of the excitement of his fifth birthday, however, there was no joy in his eyes as Royce returned to the living room empty-handed. He was troubled about something. That was apparent to both Royce and Penny.

"What is it, Craig?" his dad asked, reaching out affectionately and rumpling his hair. "This is your birthday. Don't you even have a smile for us?"

The boy looked up. For an instant he seemed to want to smile, but something kept his face clouded and his lips trembling.

"What is it, Craig?" Penny asked tenderly.

Now he would have to say it. He was suddenly embarrassed.

"I—I—" He swallowed at the lump that would not leave his throat. "I want to go over and live with Aunt Martha."

Both Penny and Royce stared at him incredulously.

"But why?" his dad asked. "What makes you say that?"

There was a brief, tortured silence.

He gritted his teeth, eyes flashing darkly.

"Aunt Martha told me that you're going to have a new baby come to live at our house."

"That's right," Royce told him. "We were going to tell you about it tonight. We think it's wonderful and thought you would be happy about it too."

For the moment Penny was too stunned to speak. She had never supposed that they would get a reaction like that from Craig.

Once he opened the subject the words came tumbling out. "Aunt Martha said that after the baby comes you won't love me or anything." Tears escaped his eyelashes and trickled down his cheeks. "She said I could come over and live at her house. So that's what I'm going to do. I'm not going to stay here anymore!"

Briefly Royce and Penny stared at Craig. Then Penny knelt beside his chair and wrapped him in her arms.

"Oh, Craig," she murmured tearfully, "don't *ever* think anything like that. Daddy and I could never get along without you."

"But you'll have the new baby," he repeated, his young voice breaking. "You won't want me anymore after *he* comes here to live."

"Don't you ever think the new baby will take your place," she tried to assure him. "I'm going to have to have you help me take care of our baby. He'll be your baby too."

Penny went on to tell him how nice it would be to have a

60

baby brother or sister, how much fun they could have playing together, and the things he could do as the big brother.

"You know, big brothers are somebody mighty special," she concluded. "One of the reasons we wanted to have a little baby was because of you."

Gradually the tremor in Craig's lips ceased and he was smiling again as he started to open his packages. By bedtime he was as happy as though the incident had never taken place at all.

When he was finally asleep, a chubby arm wrapped about the new ball he got for his birthday, Royce motioned Penny into the kitchen.

"That came from Martha Laird!" he exploded. "Craig would never have thought of anything like that on his own."

The hurt gleamed in Penny's blue eyes.

"We should have told him about the new baby," she said.

"We should have prepared him for this before anyone else had a chance to talk with him. If she hadn't filled him full of nonsense about our not loving him anymore with a new baby in the house, he'd have been happy about it, as happy as most kids his age are at the prospect of a new baby in the family."

"I know."

Royce stormed across the room and whirled to stand before the refrigerator, eyes blazing.

"I'm going over and have it out with that woman!" he exclaimed. "This isn't going to happen again!"

Penny was working her hands nervously, but it was some time before she spoke again.

"Please don't, Royce," she said, her voice quavering. "That won't solve anything. It'll just make her all the more determined that we are mistreating Craig. It'll only make matters worse!"

"But we can't let her get away with this! She's turning our own son against us!"

Penny moved quietly over to him and slipped a small, slim arm about his waist.

"We'll just have to take special effort to prove to him that what she's been telling him is all wrong. We've got to demonstrate our love to him so unmistakably he can't possibly doubt it, regardless of what anyone says to him."

For a time Penny kept Craig from going over to Martha Laird's. Whenever he wanted to go and visit the older woman, she would talk him out of it by playing a game with him, or reading to him, or telling stories. But, as the time for the baby's arrival approached, she was too exhausted to put forth such effort. Indeed, although she would have denied it at the time, she was glad for the few moments when Craig would go over to Mrs. Laird's to play. It would give her a chance to lie down for a few minutes or read a magazine.

One afternoon shortly before Penny was to go to the hospital Mrs. Laird appeared at the door and announced that she would be glad to take care of Craig during her confinement.

"Thank you," Penny said, "but Royce has already talked with Aunt Sally. She'll be coming to spend a couple of weeks with us when the baby is born."

"I see." Martha Laird drew herself up haughtily, as though Penny had slapped her across the mouth. "I'm sorry I bothered you. I was only trying to help."

The following week six-and-a-half-pound Becky put in her appearance. When Royce brought Penny and the new baby home from the hospital, Craig seemed to be as proud of her as either of his parents.

"We have a new baby at our house," he would tell people on the street as they went by. "Do you want to come in and see her?"

7

ONCE THE ROUTINE of having a new baby in the house was established, Royce started having family devotions at the breakfast table and had Craig start to learn Bible verses. Although he was only five, he seemed to enjoy that, especially when Penny helped him with them. Perching on a stool while she bathed the baby, he would repeat the verses he was learning. It wasn't long until he knew quite a list of them and, with the proper inducement, would say them all.

Royce and Penny were faithful in attending their own Sunday school and morning services, but they were also regular in attendance at the neighboring church on Sunday nights. It wasn't long until they began to question some of the things their new minister was preaching.

Royce was the first to mention it.

"He keeps talking about Jesus being the great example," he said. "He doesn't say anything about Jesus Christ, the Saviour, and he doesn't use the Bible the way they do over at the Community Church."

"I've been thinking the same thing," Penny told him. She didn't explain that she had been praying he would begin to see the differences in the preaching.

Royce stood erect.

"I wonder if it would do any good to go and talk with him about it some time."

Penny was silent. There were times when she did not understand this husband of hers. Painfully shy most of the time, he would, on occasion, do or say things few would have the courage to do. There was a stubborn streak in him and an impetuous nature that caused him to rush in where a more cautious individual would hesitate. Like going to Crandall. She hoped he wouldn't. She knew it wouldn't do any good. Royce might forget all about it and never mention it again. But she knew that if he decided it should be done, nothing she could say would stop him.

*   *   *

Becky changed rapidly with the passing months. She was as small and delicate as Craig was large—a slight, blonde bundle of energy that was seldom still. She walked at nine months and was putting words together before she was two years old.

There was little of Royce that was apparent in the blue-eyed coquette. She was bold where he was shy, vivacious and lively where he was quiet and often moody. Perhaps that was why she was able to get such a hold upon his heart. He saw in her the shortcomings of his own personality. Or, perhaps his was only the love a man had for his daughter and Royce, who knew the bitter taste of death, was more sensitive to it, allowing himself to feel a bit more deeply.

Becky and Craig got on well together as they grew older, in spite of the fact that he teased her constantly. He would grab her by the arm and hold her until she cried, or put his foot against the bathroom door and refuse to let her out until her screams of frustration and anger brought Penny running. She scolded him and punished him by making him go to his room, and later by spanking, but it seemed to have little effect on him.

"I can't understand it, Royce," she said when they were alone in their bedroom at night. "Craig and Becky seem to love each other as much as any brother and sister, but he teases her constantly. He doesn't seem satisfied unless he has her crying."

A smile tugged upward at the corners of his mouth.

"I seem to remember a lot of fighting I used to do with

my brothers and sisters," he said, "and doing a lot of teasing in between. I think the teasing is half the fun of having sisters."

"We used to tease a lot too," she acknowledged, "but I never remember any of us carrying it as far as Craig does. When he starts he won't quit until she's in tears."

"I'll talk to him about it if you want me to."

Penny lay silently in the crook of his arm for a minute or two.

"I don't think talking to him will do any good," she said at last. "I've been wondering if we're spending enough time with him. Maybe this is his way of demanding attention."

Royce didn't agree with her.

"I play ball with him for a while practically every noon," he told her, "at least when the weather's nice. And we have a game of checkers every night or spend some time reading out loud to him. I can't see that it's lack of attention that making him like he is."

"He needs more of our time than the average child," she insisted. "I suppose it's the loss of his mother that's caused him to be so insecure, but he seems to need the assurance that we love him."

Royce was ready to write the matter off. Because he knew Craig was loved and wanted, he was inclined to assume that his son knew it too. Not so with Penny; she was still disturbed.

"A boy needs to spend some time alone with his dad," she continued. "Do you suppose you could give him some special attention on Saturdays, Royce? Could the two of you do something special together?"

He thought about that. Penny couldn't be right about Craig not thinking he was wanted and loved, but the prospect of spending more time with his son appealed to him. He enjoyed those periods of playing ball and checkers almost as much as Craig did.

"I probably couldn't give him every Saturday afternoon, but I should be able to spend quite a few Saturday afternoons with him."

He didn't know exactly what he would do on Saturday that Craig would find interesting. Playing that much ball would probably get tiresome, and there was no zoo to go to. But he ought to be able to come up with something.

He said nothing to Craig about it until the following Saturday at noon. They were sitting at the table when he turned to his son.

"Got anything planned for the rest of the day, Craig?"

"Can I go, Daddy?" Becky broke in before Craig had time to answer. "Can I go?"

"I was talking to your brother."

Craig made a face at her.

"I don't know," he said. "I was just going to fool around."

"How about going out in the country with me?"

"Can I go?" Becky persisted. "Can I, Daddy? Can I?"

"Not this time, honey. This is just for Craig and me."

Until that moment Craig hadn't acted interested. That seemed to settle it for him. He brightened noticeably.

"What'll we do?"

It was Royce's turn to hesitate. He had done a great deal of thinking about that, but hadn't come up with the answer to it himself.

"We could go for a ride."

Craig groaned.

"In a car?" he asked with all the enthusiasm of being invited to play with dolls.

"Can you think of anything better to ride?"

He squinted up at him speculatively. "A pony."

That was something Royce would have to talk him out of, and he didn't know just how. After all, he had asked Craig what he wanted to ride. Then he remembered a farmer friend who had a couple of Shetland ponies. He had been building a new house and came to Royce with a problem or two that he hadn't charged for answering. He had told Royce that if there was ever anything he could do for him to let him know.

"I just might be able to fix you up, at that." He turned to the phone.

"Do you mean it, Dad?" Craig's eyes danced expectantly.

Harry was home when Royce called and was glad to have

him bring his son out to ride one of the Shetlands. He put the most gentle of the two in the barn and had her saddled by the time Royce and Craig drove into the yard.

The boy advanced hesitantly toward the pony, as though she would disappear or turn and flee the barn if he moved too close, too rapidly.

He stopped just short of the Shetland and turned to Royce, his voice still hushed with awe.

"Is it all right if I touch her, Dad?" he wanted to know.

"Sure. Go ahead."

Dreamily Craig stepped forward and touched the Shetland mare on the withers. She flinched and he drew his hand away.

"That's all right," Harry told him. "Take hold of her bridle and lead her outside."

Craig ran his fingers gently along the pony's neck to the reins.

"There now," he murmured softly. "I'm not going to hurt you."

He led the pony outside, still enchanted by this wonderful thing that was happening to him. Royce's smile spread across his face as he saw the happiness glinting in Craig's eyes.

The Shetland was well broken and Craig seemed to have a way with her from the first moment he pulled himself clumsily into the saddle. It wasn't long until he was riding at a brisk trot down the lane while Royce watched proudly.

He and Craig had a better time together that afternoon than he could ever remember. It was past dinnertime and dark when they came back to town. They were both tired and dirty, but their faces were radiant.

"Oh, Mom!" Craig cried, bursting into the kitchen. "You should've been there!" Excitement widened his eyes and caused his voice to crescendo. "You should've been there!"

Penny bent to kiss his dirt-stained face.

"You sound as though you had a good time."

His gaze met hers triumphantly.

"I rode the pony all around the yard without anybody

67

holding onto me or anything!" He stopped and turned to Royce. "Didn't I, Daddy?"

"You certainly did."

He came back to where Royce had sat down near the table.

"Will you get me a pony, Daddy?" he asked.

Royce was slow in replying to him.

"It's not too easy to take care of a horse in town, Craig," he tried to explain.

"I'd take care of him. You wouldn't have to worry about that. I'd take care of him all the time. You'd never have to feed him or anything."

"We'll have to see about that."

Craig accepted that answer for a time, but Royce knew he was going to have to answer him again and again. When he got something like that in mind he was not easily dissuaded.

After that it was a regular event for Royce and Craig to go out to the farm on Saturday afternoon to ride. After a time Royce made arrangements for one of Harry's saddle horses for himself, and he and Craig went for long rides together.

Those were happy, carefree occasions, and Craig seemed better adjusted than ever. He seldom went to see Martha Laird anymore. With school, playing catch with his dad and their long rides every Saturday afternoon, there was little time for visiting.

Then Penny became pregnant again.

"What are we going to do about telling Craig?" she asked Royce almost as soon as they were sure of the approaching event themselves.

He hesitated. "We won't have to tell him for a little while, will we?"

"We don't want Mrs. Laird to do it for us again."

Concern gleamed in Royce's eyes. If people like Martha Laird would just leave Craig alone they wouldn't have quite so many problems with him. Why did they have to consider

Mrs. Laird at every turn? Why couldn't she keep out of it? Why did she think she had to interfere?

The day Penny went to the doctor for the first time they called Craig into the living room and told him about the new baby. His resentment glimmered.

"What's the matter?" he demanded, lips curling. "Aren't Becky and me enough? Why do we have to have a new baby anyway?"

They did not answer him directly.

"Wouldn't you like to have a baby brother?" Royce asked him.

Craig's firm lips twisted. That was something he hadn't considered. In a way a little brother would be all right. He'd have somebody besides Dad to play catch with, and— He glanced uneasily at Penny. In spite of that, he didn't think he liked the idea. The more he considered it the more sure he was that he wasn't going to like it.

"We don't need anyone else!" he retorted, his lower lip quivering. "Everything's OK just as it is."

Exasperation and anger smoked across Royce's taut face.

"Well, we're having another baby," he said sternly. "That's all there is to it. You'll just have to get used to the idea."

Penny's quick look silenced him. She put an arm about Craig and drew him close. At first he held back as though he didn't want her caress, but she knew that in the deep recesses of his heart, he wanted her—needed her, at this particular moment.

"God sends us babies when He thinks we ought to have them," she told him as gently as possible. "We can't doubt God. We can't think He makes mistakes, can we, Craig?"

He considered her statement, the frown lines across his forehead deepening.

"I—I suppose not." His tone revealed that he was giving her the answer he knew she wanted to hear and not what he believed himself.

After a time he turned to Royce.

"This won't mean that we have to quit going out to the farm to go horseback riding, does it, Dad?"

"I don't see why it should."

Craig sensed that the conversation was over and backed away.

"I don't know why you want another squalling baby around here anyway," he exclaimed over his shoulder. "We've got enough kids in this family."

Royce thought little about the incident after that. Craig would get over his resentment. He had with Becky, except for the way he teased her. It would be the same with this new baby. He was getting older too, and that would make a difference.

However, the following week when he came home from the office Penny and Craig were sitting in the living room eyeing each other. Both faces were serious, but Craig's cheeks were stained with tears and defiance still glinted faintly in his eyes.

Royce saw there was something wrong the instant he opened the door.

"Say, now." He came in, looking from one to the other. "What's going on here? What's the trouble?"

Neither of them answered.

He had had a good day at work and was in a warm, expansive mood.

"It can't be as bad as all that."

The silence lengthened between them. Craig squirmed uncomfortably and Penny looked as though she was about to cry.

"What is this?" Royce asked. "What's wrong?"

"Craig has something to tell you."

The boy fumbled gloomily with the words.

"You tell him."

"No," she retorted. "You are to tell him. That was our understanding. Remember?"

Craig swallowed at the lump that rose in his throat.

"It's nothing to get so shook up about," he said defensively. "All I did was throw some clods at some stupid old girls and the teacher caught me and made me stay after school. That's all."

With difficulty Royce kept from smiling. He hoped Craig didn't guess that he was laughing inwardly at it. He couldn't help it. It reminded him of an incident that happened back home when he was a kid. He supposed almost every boy had gotten into trouble for throwing things at girls at one time or another.

"You know you shouldn't have done that, don't you?"

"I didn't hurt them none! All I did was hit her on the arm. And she had to go screaming to the teacher like she was killed or something."

"Craig," Penny broke in sternly, "that's not what the note from the teacher said."

His cheeks colored and for an instant or two he was subdued.

"Now," Penny continued, "suppose you tell us what actually happened."

Defiance flamed high in the boy's eyes.

"How many times do I have to tell you? I just threw some clods at some stupid old girls, that's all! And they had to go and tell on me."

Royce took over when he saw that Penny wasn't able to shake Craig's story. He got no farther than his wife had. Craig's lower lip shot out and his lips narrowed as he spat out the words savagely. There wasn't anything else to tell except that he had thrown some clods at some girls and they told on him. It was all their fault. When he refused to say more Royce ordered him to his room.

"I haven't had any supper," Craig protested.

"Perhaps going without supper will help teach you to behave yourself."

The boy went storming into his room.

Some time after dinner that evening Royce went in to talk to him. Craig was lying on the bed, eyes open, staring belligerently up at the ceiling.

"All I did was throw some clods at some stupid old girls," he muttered.

Royce sat on the edge of the bed.

71

"You know this wasn't the first time, don't you?" he said. Craig did not answer him.

"Your teacher said that she has punished you several times for it herself, and that this time you hit a girl in the face and almost hit her eye."

"It wasn't that bad," he muttered.

"We don't want you to be a bad boy, Craig. We want you to be good and have people like you."

The boy's young face clouded.

"What do you care? You've got Mother and Becky to love, and now you're going to have another baby. You don't care about *me* anymore."

"But we do," Royce protested. "We love you a great deal, Craig."

The boy's lips quavered. "Mother doesn't."

"What makes you say that?"

No answer.

Royce's voice grim. "Did Aunt Martha Laird tell you that?"

Craig hesitated.

"The kids at school say it too. They say I've got a step-mother!" A venom Royce had never heard before in Craig's voice laced his words.

*   *   *

Royce and Penny had been determined that this new pregnancy would not change things as far as Craig and their relationships with him were concerned. They were going to give him just as much time and attention as they had before. They were going to show him by their actions they loved him and were concerned about his happiness and welfare.

However, it was inevitable that there were certain adjustments to be made. For one thing Penny wasn't feeling well much of the time. And, as weeks progressed, she found it increasingly difficult to take care of the house and her family and still have time to devote to Craig. In spite of all her intentions there were certain compromises between desire and reality that she had to make. And when she was sick on Saturday Royce felt that he had to help at home, even though

72

it meant giving up the afternoon of horseback riding with Craig.

"But you promised!" Craig protested. "You promised, Dad."

Royce knew how badly his son wanted to go horseback riding. He knew how much he looked forward to it each Saturday afternoon. Those hours on the farm were the crowning event of the week. Royce didn't like to break his word to Craig, but he couldn't always help it.

"Mother isn't feeling too well today, Craig," he would try to explain. "I've got to take care of Becky and help around the house."

Craig eyed him sullenly and without understanding.

"I wish it was just you and me, Dad," he exclaimed with unexpected bitterness. "Then we could go horseback riding every Saturday and not have to stay home and take care of anybody. We could do anything we wanted to do."

"But we wouldn't have anybody to cook for us," Royce tried to explain, "or clean our clothes or keep the house nice."

The boy's lower lip shot out petulantly.

"Aunt Martha would have done it, if you'd asked her," he countered. "She told me she would have."

Royce studied him, eyes narrowing. This wasn't his son talking; these were the words of a lonely, bitter, misunderstanding woman.

"I don't want you to go over and see Mrs. Laird any more, Craig," he ordered. "Do you understand?"

The boy's head came up, eyes blazing their defiance, as though to shout to Royce that he would go over and see Mrs. Laird if he wanted to.

"I'll tell you what I'll do," Royce continued, trying not to let his son see how much this new attitude disturbed him, "next Saturday we'll go horseback riding for sure."

"Promise?"

"Even if we have to hire a sitter for Becky."

That seemed to make Craig feel a little better and Royce wondered if his anger and resentment might only be on the

73

surface. Now that he thought about it he realized that was the way it had to be. Craig had thought too much of Penny for too many years to turn on her so suddenly.

The next Saturday afternoon Penny was feeling as uncomfortable as she had all week. Still, she insisted that she was able to keep Becky.

"We can get one of the neighbor girls to look after her," Royce said.

"Oh no, I'm fine." She brushed her hair back from her face with a weary hand.

"We'll try to be back early," he whispered as he kissed her good-bye.

He thought he had spoken softly enough to avoid being overheard but Craig had been listening intently for just such a remark.

"Oh no we won't," he protested belligerently. "We're going to stay late. We're going to stay awful late! You promised!"

Although he was speaking to his dad he was staring coldly at Penny as though she was his adversary in the battle for his dad's time and affection. Penny felt it and looked away quickly to keep them both from seeing her tears.

On their ride that afternoon Royce guided the conversation to the topic of God. He had been wanting to talk to Craig about his relationship with God for some time. On other occasions he had tried to talk with him about his need of Christ, but he had never been able to make any solid progress. There were occasions when he was sure his son understood and had made a decision to walk with Christ. Other times doubts pried in.

"Do you ever think about God, Craig?" he asked, deliberately holding his voice to a conversational level.

The boy tightened his grip on the reins.

"Sometimes."

"You know, each of us needs God, Craig," Royce continued, trying to plan some effective way of saying what he felt so deeply himself. It wasn't easy talking about such things with his own son. He could talk with him about school or baseball or horses with no problem at all, but if he started to mention Christ and Craig's relationship with Him, the words caught in his throat and he was suddenly warm and perspiring. He didn't know why it had to be that way, but it did. With the one person he was more concerned about than anyone else, he found his tongue strangely tied.

"I don't need anybody to look out for me," Craig blurted. "I can take care of myself."

They crossed the road and turned in at the lane before Royce answered him.

"Nobody can take care of himself, Craig. I found that out a long time ago. God knew that we couldn't take care of ourselves without living terrible lives of sin, so He sent Jesus Christ so we could believe on Him and have our sin forgiven and go to heaven."

Craig formed the words slowly.

"I'm going to be the same kind of a Christian Don Wells is," he said.

Royce's eyebrows arched.

"Who's Don Wells?"

"My Sunday school teacher."

Something about the boy's tone caused Royce to question him further.

"What makes you say you want to be the same kind of Christian Mr. Wells is?"

Craig's gaze narrowed darkly.

"He does anything he wants to."

8

Royce did not say anything for a time to Penny about Craig's curt appraisal of his Sunday school teacher's spiritual qualifications, but he thought much about it.

Perhaps that was one of his son's problems. He and Penny were trying to guide him in one direction; the church where they were members was leading in another. People were teaching Sunday school over there who shouldn't be teachers at all. Their lives were so far short of what they should be that even kids like Craig could see the incongruity of it. How could he and Penny expect Craig to be what he should be when a man like this Wells was teaching his Sunday school class?

Something had to be done, he reasoned. But what?

Penny voiced the same question when he finally shared the problem with her.

"What can we do about it?" she asked.

He sat down heavily, clasping his hands so tightly his knuckles whitened.

"I've wrestled with this thing for two weeks, Penny," he said. "And as I see it, there's only one thing we can do.

We can't change the whole church. All we can do is to start going to a church where we agree with what is being taught."

Penny fell silent. She had been forced to fight for acceptance at the church where they were going now. It had not been easy to come into a wealthy church with the socially prominent and win a place for herself. But she had accomplished it although it had taken three years. Now she was put on committees with the wives of the town's lawyers and doctors and bankers as casually as though she was one of them. If she was honest with herself, she had to admit that she enjoyed it. She found it exciting to go into the town's largest and most beautiful homes for meetings and to be seen in the company of the women who lived in them.

There were other times when those same women made her feel inferior, so unworthy, that she felt she could not go back there to church; when she felt she was still the poor fatherless little girl who had to bring a jar of pickles to the school picnic because her mother didn't have the required fifteen cents for refreshments.

That was all the more reason she was reluctant to make the change. She knew what they would do and say. She knew how she and Royce would be treated once their decision to change churches became known.

Not that it really mattered, she told herself. Actually, those things should be of no concern to her. The important thing was to be in a church where the Bible was taught and where it was expressed in the lives of the people, and especially in the lives of those teaching Sunday school classes. She was ashamed of herself for her hesitation. Still, she felt that she had to mention the problems that such a move would bring.

"You know it's not going to be easy for us to do that and stay in Glenville, Royce," she told him quietly.

He did not answer her.

"A good many of the town's most important people go there and they love their church. They're not going to accept our leaving too kindly."

His gaze met hers.

"Are you with me in this matter, Penny?" he demanded, his voice coarsening.

"Of course I am."

He drew in a deep breath.

"Then that's all that matters. We stand together."

Her smile was thin and crooked.

"We stand together," she said, "but I think I ought to tell you now that I'm not very brave."

"Neither am I. But if you're willing to take it, Penny, we'll make the change."

She slipped into the crook of his arm and looked up at him.

"You know I'm with you in whatever you feel we should do, Royce."

Neither of them had supposed it would make any difference to Craig, but it seemed to.

"I don't know any of the kids over at Community Church or anything," he protested. "I want to keep going to my old Sunday school."

"You'll get acquainted," Penny told him.

He eyed her resentfully.

"My *mother* went to our Sunday school," he reminded them caustically. "And that's where I'm going. I'm not going to change."

Royce's eyes flashed.

"And who told you that your mother used to go to the church we're leaving, Craig?" he demanded.

"She did go to our Sunday school, didn't she?"

"Yes," Royce replied, "she did. But who told you that she did?"

"Aunt Martha said she used to be in Sunday school and church every Sunday." His young voice rose defensively. "I want to go to my mother's Sunday school. I don't want to go to a different one."

Royce did not try to explain his reasons for the change to Craig. He had not been able to make Crandall, the new minister, or the church board understand why they had to leave. How could he explain it to Craig? He would have

78

to leave the matter and hope his son would fully understand it when he got older.

They started going to the Community Church the following Sunday. A boy in Craig's grade took him down to class and introduced him to the others. He was surprised to find that he enjoyed it, although he didn't say anything to his folks about it. And when they asked him, he pretended that he hated every minute.

Staying for the morning service was something else again. The service was somewhat longer than it had been where they used to go, for one thing. The message at their former church had never been more than twenty minutes long, and the service itself a scant hour. At Community Church the service was less formal and, as a result, ran overtime on occasion. Another thing Craig didn't like was that the kids were expected to sit with their parents. It was more fun when he could get with two or three other guys in one corner and whisper.

It wasn't long after they changed churches that the twins were born. Penny started having pains in the middle of the night and by seven o'clock the next morning the family had been increased by two. Royce sat on the edge of Craig's bed and told him about it.

"Now you'll have two baby brothers to play with," he said.

Disapproval twisted Craig's face, but he did not give voice to it. He seldom expressed his own feelings in words anymore, but held them grimly in check. Still, his eyes and the deepening lines in his young face revealed what his lack of words would have hidden.

"Isn't it wonderful?" his dad asked.

"I guess so."

He was curious enough to see the babies, and asked Royce about them several times. But when Penny came home from the hospital with them he refused to look in their cribs. That night when it came time for him to go to bed he insisted that Penny read to him and hear his prayers.

"Don't you want to have me do it for you, Craig?" Royce asked.

"You don't read good enough. I want Mother to do it."

Royce started to protest that Mother was tired, but Penny stopped him with a quick, expressive gleam in her eyes.

"You go get the book, Craig," she told him. "I'll read to you."

He scooted away. A moment later he was back, triumphantly climbing on her lap.

Later that night he got sick and cried for Penny. His dad went in to see what was wrong with him.

"Can't I help you?"

"My stomach hurts," Craig moaned. "Mother is the one who knows what to do for it."

"I'll go and ask her, OK?"

But that didn't satisfy Craig.

"You don't know what to do for a stomach that hurts," he said scornfully.

Penny got Craig a drink of water and half an aspirin.

"It'll feel better in a little while, honey."

His eyes searched hers, pleading.

"I think it would feel better if you rubbed it."

She sat down on the bed and for several minutes rubbed his stomach. Impulsively he threw his arms about her neck and drew her down to him. For half a minute or so, he clung to her.

Penny was in the boy's room so long Royce thought something was wrong and came to the door to look in on them, but she warned him away with her eyes. It was half an hour or so later before she came back to bed.

Royce was irritated.

"You shouldn't let him work you that way, Penny," he said. "I don't think he was sick at all. He just wanted you to be in there with him."

"He needed me, Royce," she said simply, a note of joy in her voice. "He had to think of some excuse to keep me with him."

It was inevitable, however, that Penny would have less

time to devote to Craig in the weeks and months that followed. Becky was still quite small and had to be cared for, and with twins it seemed that her work was never done. She was most concerned about the fact that she could not spend as much time as she would like to spend with their oldest son. As it was, she stole minutes from other things to play games or read to him. He acted starved for her love and affection, yet he didn't seem to know how to respond to it. He would scowl boyishly when she put her arm about him, and try to draw away, but Penny could read the desperate longing in his eyes.

"I'm so sorry I'm not able to spend all the time with Craig that I ought to," she told Royce.

"You give him more time than most mothers with other kids are able to give their oldest sons," he reminded her.

"But he needs me so very much."

Royce didn't say anything in reply, but he couldn't understand how Craig could possibly need Penny more than other kids needed their mothers.

She was already doing too much. She wasn't as strong as most women her age, weighing less than a hundred pounds. And with Craig and three other little ones to take care of, she had all she could do to keep up with the work, let alone spend hours on end with Craig.

"He'll just have to get along without as much of your time as he'd like to have for a little while, Penny," Royce told her. "Other boys have to get along without the full attention and time of their mothers."

* * *

It wasn't long until Craig was old enough to go to young people's meetings on Sunday night an hour before the evening church service. At first he went without protest, but it was only a short time until he began to try in every way possible to avoid it.

"I'm not feeling good tonight, Dad," he would say, his face twisting expressively. "I don't think I ought to go to young people's tonight."

Or he would have some studies that simply had to be finished by the first period on Monday morning.

Gradually Royce began to see through the subterfuge.

"It isn't going to do any good for you to argue with me," he said firmly. "You're going to young people's tonight. That's all there is to it."

The other guys don't have to go unless they want to," Craig retorted, scowling darkly.

"That's between them and their folks," Royce said. "This is between you and me."

The boy glared belligerently. "I don't know why I've got to go to church all the time," he grumbled. "When I get big I'm not going. I can tell you that much right now."

"Until you're grown and living in your own home, you'll do as we say," Royce reminded him.

And that ended the argument. He would let Craig say no more about it. He drove Craig to the church and let him out.

"Mother and I will be along in time for the services," he said. "We'll expect you to stay for church tonight."

"For cryin' out loud!"

Royce drove several blocks in the direction of their home after letting Craig out when a vague uneasiness enveloped him. His son started up the steps of the church as though he was going straight inside, but there had been something disturbing about his manner. Royce didn't know exactly why he was concerned, or why he doubted Craig's intentions, for that matter, but at the next corner he made a U-turn and went back. Sure enough, a block from the church he saw Craig, walking briskly in the direction of the Glenville business district.

Craig recognized the car, but not soon enough to hide. Royce swung over to the curb and stopped beside him. Craig saw that he was caught and swaggered brazenly over to the car.

"I thought you were going to young people's," Royce said, anger flecking his voice.

"I was," Craig explained, lying easily, "but the meeting

had already started when I got there. I didn't want every-body staring at me, so I didn't go in."

Royce's temper flared. There were many things Craig did that he could overlook, but lying was not one of them. He was furious.

"Craig, when I let you out in front of the church it was exactly twenty-five minutes after 6." He looked at his watch. "It isn't even 6:30 yet and the meetings never start before 6:30."

The boy went around to the other side of the car and got in beside him, but anger and defiance were in every move.

"I get tired of having to go to church all the time," he growled. "Other kids don't have to keep going whether they want to or not. I don't see why I have to."

Royce did not start the car immediately.

"What's the trouble, Craig?" he asked, even more serious than before. "Why do you keep doing the things you do?"

His son glared at him, but did not answer.

"What is it, Craig?" he repeated.

His scowl deepened.

"I don't see why it couldn't just be you and me, Dad!" he exploded. "Everything would be all right if it was. It's all *her* fault!"

"Do you mean Mother?" Royce asked.

The boy's lower lip trembled.

"I don't have a mother!"

9

THE TWINS CHANGED RAPIDLY in the months that followed.
One day Penny had brought them home from the hospital.
The next day, or so it seemed to Royce, they were crawling
across the floor. They were as small and wiry as Craig had
been large, and it wasn't long until they were walking everywhere. Another day or two and they were beginning to talk.

Becky adored them. By this time she had started school
and was continually informing the teacher about the cute
things her twin baby brothers were doing. She would stop
playing dolls or come home from the neighbors any time
just for the privilege of helping take care of them.

Craig ignored the twins pointedly. If one or the other
toddled up to him, as they often did at first, he would scowl
and turn his back on them. Or, if Penny and Royce were in
the room to scold him for it, he pushed them away. They
soon learned to leave him alone.

His attitude toward the twins was of great concern to
Royce and Penny. They talked with him about it often, trying to make him see that the boys were his brothers and
he should love them. But it had little effect on him; he still
acted as though they didn't exist.

84

His relationship with Becky, however, did not change. He teased her until the tears coursed down her round little cheeks and she would scream her defiance at him until Penny rushed to see what was the matter. Or, if they were alone, she would kick him on the shins hard enough to raise welts and make him limp. But there was a bond between them that seemed to grow stronger as they grew older. This was reassuring to their parents.

Craig seemed little different than the other boys his age during those formative years, except that he spent more time alone and had fewer friends than most. Royce thought it was because he was self-conscious at being bigger than anyone else in his class. He towered over all of them, including the teacher, a gangling, awkward lad who stumbled frequently, and he had difficulty in playing football or basketball with his smaller, better coordinated classmates. He soon gave up trying to play either sport.

Craig was in that difficult period of change and awakening. The little boy was still there, soft and pliable, and hungry for affection, but the teenager's moody restlessness and rebellion was taking hold of him. His smoky blue eyes revealed the turmoil that was seizing him, the surging emotions that lifted him to the skies or plunged him into deep depression without apparent reason.

Royce and Penny saw that he got to young people's and Sunday school, but he made no attempt to hide the fact that he was there only because he had to be. If there was a disturbance in class it could usually be traced to him. His grades at school were not good in spite of the fact that his I.Q. indicated a nimble mind.

"Craig would do much better if he applied himself," his instructors wrote on the bottom of his report card.

"He does not pay attention to directions, has poor attitude."

"He doesn't seem to want to study, nor allow anyone else near him to study either."

When he brought home a report card, he knew that his

folks were going to talk with him about it and he steeled himself for the lecture that was sure to come.

"The teachers have got it in for me," he would tell them defensively. "They give me poor grades because they don't like me."

"I'm sure that's not true," Royce countered.

"It is so true. If you don't believe it, ask the other kids. They'll tell you. It doesn't make any difference how hard I try, I don't get credit for anything I do."

Royce insisted that he bring his books home and study each evening before he did anything else. Belligerence smoking in his surly eyes, Craig agreed, but it was a reluctant, forced agreement. He brought them home for a time and made a pretense of studying; but as soon as the pressure was relaxed slightly, he quit even that.

"Yes, I've got my lessons," he would break in when Royce started to ask him about his studies and his grades. "For cryin' out loud! Can't you give a guy a break? All I ever hear around here is static about studying or cleaning my room or taking out the trash! I'm getting fed up!"

"That's enough, Craig!" Royce was stern.

Craig fell silent, but anger and resentment smoldered ominously in his eyes. He seemed to hate authority, and at times it seemed to Royce that Craig hated both him and Penny, as well.

But, regardless of what happened, Becky idolized Craig and was fiercely loyal to him.

"I'll go and get your books," she would volunteer, scurrying for his basement room. "I'll get you some notebook paper."

He seemed to enjoy having her run errands for him. That bothered Royce too. He was getting more self-centered every day.

* * *

Craig was in the tenth grade when Royce was called to the school by the principal. He wanted to ask what it was about, but by the time he framed the question the phone

86

call was over. He started to phone Penny to tell her about it, but changed his mind and hung up without dialing the number. There was nothing she could do about it. He might as well wait to tell her until he found out exactly what was wrong.

When Royce arrived, his son was sitting in Mr. Ellsworth's office, slouched in a chair with exaggerated indifference to what was going on about him. Royce had seen that look on Craig's face before. Fear flecked his eyes, but he tried hard to mask it by looking at them with amused superiority, as though he was beyond being affected by anything they might say or do.

"I've been hesitating to call you, Mr. Lawson," the principal began, closing the door to his outer office and lowering his voice to keep anyone else from hearing, "but finally the situation got to the place where something had to be done."

"I see." He glanced at Craig. The fear was there, all right, and growing in intensity. He squirmed uneasily as he felt the two men staring at him.

"You guys act as though I robbed a bank or something," he blurted.

Suddenly Royce went weak. What was it that his son had done?

"His grades have been miserable, for one thing," Mr. Ellsworth said, as though Royce had voiced the question aloud. "For another, he's been missing a great deal of school. So much that it's a wonder to me he's able to do passing work in anything."

Royce's gaze met Craig's and would not let it go. This was something he hadn't known about.

"What's this about missing school?" he demanded.

His son looked down.

"I wasn't aware that you had missed any time at all."

"I—I've been sick a couple of times, I guess," Craig mumbled.

The principal opened the drawer in his desk and pulled out a sheet of paper.

"Let's see, the first quarter you missed three half days

87

and four full days. The next quarter you missed six full days and two half days."

Royce stared from one to the other incredulously.

"This can't be. You haven't been sick since the first of September, Craig. Mother and I were talking about it the other night and she remarked how well you've been—that you haven't even had a cold all winter."

His son twisted and turned in his chair.

"I have the excuses in the other office," the principal continued. "As I recall they were signed by your wife."

"That's strange." The corners of Royce's mouth tightened. "Penny didn't say anything to me about signing any excuses for Craig, and especially for illness. I could understand her not telling me about his missing an afternoon, but not the number of times you have him listed as absent. May I use your phone, Mr. Ellsworth. I'd like to check this out."

"Perhaps we'd better take a look at the excuses to see if your wife actually signed them." The principal switched on the intercom. "Millie," he said to his secretary, "would you please bring me Craig Lawson's attendance file?"

"You don't need to do that," Craig broke in. "I'll tell you about it."

He eyed his dad accusingly.

"We're waiting, Craig."

"*She* wouldn't let me stay home when I was sick." His anger grew as he spoke. "When I told her I didn't feel good, she took my temperature and said it was normal so I had to go to school. She just wanted to get me out of the house, that's all. She didn't want to have me around, even when I was sick."

"And what about the excuses?"

"Mrs. Laird gave them to me."

Royce stiffened angrily.

"She signed Mother's name?" he echoed.

"I told you I was sick. I tried to tell *her* too. I was awful sick, but she wouldn't believe me." By this time he had stopped calling Penny "Mother" except on rare occasions when she had done something particularly nice for him or he was in a rare tender mood.

"So you went over to Martha Laird's and stayed, and got her to give you an excuse and sign Mother's name. Is that it?"

No answer.

"We'll talk more about this when we get home," Royce promised him.

He had already decided that he was going to have to talk to Martha Laird about shielding Craig the way she was. She would probably get mad and bawl a little, but he couldn't help it. If this continued his son wouldn't even be able to finish high school.

"There's another matter I've been wanting to talk with you about, Mr. Lawson," the principal continued. "At the basketball game last night Craig set off a firecracker in the crowded gym."

Craig grinned.

"It's no laughing matter, I can assure you," Mr. Ellsworth retorted coldly. "It caused near panic. A couple of hundred people crowded toward the exits before we were able to get them quiet. One woman was knocked down and a little boy was badly bruised. Fortunately no one was seriously hurt, but it could have happened."

"I was just trying to have a little fun."

"It wouldn't have been so funny if someone had been killed."

Mr. Ellsworth and Royce and Craig discussed the matter at length. Finally it was decided that his son would be placed on probation and lose all of his privileges except the right to go to classes and the study hall and the library. He could attend none of the athletic events or extracurricular activities.

"And if there is one more incident," the principal promised sternly, "we'll have no choice except to expel you. Is that clear?"

"I guess so." The surly, pouting grin scarcely faded from his face. Whatever he might be thinking, it was apparent that he wanted to leave the impression that he was not going to be hurt by the punishment the school was imposing.

"It had better be, if you want to continue to attend this school. That's a promise."

"It sounds fair to me," Royce told him.

Once the principal finished with Craig he sent him back to class. "But I'd like to talk with you privately, Mr. Lawson," he said, "if you have a little more time."

Royce stayed behind. Actually, he wanted to talk with the principal too. There were some things he had to find out about Craig. He wasn't sure that the principal had the answers or not, but he had to see.

Mr. Ellsworth's face was grave as he closed the door behind Craig and came back to his desk.

"I've felt for some time that I should talk with you," he began. "And not only because of some of these things that have been happening." He stopped momentarily and Royce waited without saying anything until he went on. "I'm not at all sure that we're going to be able to give Craig the sort of help he needs."

Royce was numb and cold inside. Mr. Ellsworth sounded so impersonal and matter of fact, as though he was talking about doing an overhaul on a car or repairing somebody's refrigerator. He felt like grabbing the principal by the shoulders and shaking him until he became aware of what he was talking about. It might be a part of his job to Mr. Ellsworth, but to Royce it was his son!

Don't you know this is Craig you're talking about so coldly? he demanded inwardly. *This is my son! How can you be so nerveless? How can you care so little?*

Aloud Royce spoke more gently.

"I don't believe I follow you."

"We're just not equipped to take care of a boy with the sort of problems Craig has. I'm very much afraid that it is going to take a place where they have considerably more discipline than we are able to exercise here. He may possibly need some psychiatric treatment. There are some problems in Craig's life that aren't apparent on the surface."

Royce nodded his agreement. This, he and Penny were becoming increasingly aware of.

"I know this is a personal matter, Mr. Lawson," the principal continued, "and one that I hesitate to mention, but Craig has talked with me a number of times about the way things are at home. He seems to feel that he has an impossible home situation."

Royce jerked erect. This wasn't true. Penny and he had been more concerned about Craig and showing him love and affection than they had any of the three other kids. He hadn't responded. That was all.

Mr. Ellsworth read the disagreement in Royce's face. "I'm simply repeating what he has told me," he retorted quickly. "At any rate, he is greatly disturbed emotionally. Unless something is done and done soon I am afraid you are going to have a serious problem on your hands."

Royce did not tell Penny about his conference with the school principal immediately. That is, he didn't tell her the personal portion of the interview. She felt badly enough when he told her about Craig's truancy and the incident of the firecracker in the crowded gym.

"I don't know what would have caused him to do a thing like that, Royce," she said. "We haven't raised him to be that way. We've taught him right and wrong."

It was all Royce could do to keep from telling her about the balance of his talk with Mr. Ellsworth right then. He didn't keep quiet because he didn't plan on telling her; they never kept secrets from each other. He just had to think the matter through and try to decide whether the principal was right about Craig or not.

Their son was impulsive, that was true. And he was more daring than a lot of kids. He would do things others would think of trying and might want to try, but didn't dare. Of course it was true that fellows like that were often the ones who accomplished great things in life if their courage and daring could only be directed. Craig's sensitivity and intelligence didn't help either, when it came to making him tractable and easy to handle.

Then there was his attitude toward Penny. That had probably been more disturbing to him than anything else Mr. Ellsworth said, although both he and Penny knew how Craig had come to feel about her. If anyone did not deserve such treatment for the way she played her role as stepmother, it was Penny. She loved him as fervently as she loved any of their children. If anything, she might have loved him a little more, since he needed her so much more than the others did.

What to do about Craig was another matter. He supposed they could put him in a private school, but with three smaller children that would be an expense they could ill afford.

"I think you and I hold the answer, Penny," he told her at last. "We've got to crack down on that young man. He can get decent grades if he just applies himself and stays out of trouble."

She nodded her agreement.

"We've been too lax with him. We've got to get hold of him and bring him into line."

The middle of the week Royce had another telephone call about Craig. This time it was from the police.

"We've got Craig and two of his friends down here, Royce," Joe Christy said. "We'd like to have you and Penny come down."

"What has he done?" Royce asked. He could not keep his voice from quavering.

Joe Christy found it difficult to tell him. After all, they had been friends for years. Royce knew it wasn't easy for him to take Craig into custody.

"I'd rather tell you about it when you get here."

"We'll be down just as soon as we can."

Penny was standing at Royce's elbow when he hung up. "It's about Craig, isn't it?"

"Joe wants us to come down."

She hesitated.

"Unless you'd rather I go alone," Royce told her.

"Oh, no," she said quickly. "I wouldn't think of that. I

was just trying to decide who I'd get to look after the kids while we're gone." She picked up the phone. "I'll call Hansons next door and see if Dixie is home."

As soon as the Hanson girl arrived, Royce and Penny went down to the police station. The other parents were already there when they came in. Craig was sitting alone, tears washing his eyes. When he saw them his shoulders began to tremble and his lips parted, but no sound came out.

Royce stood some distance away, but Penny went over and sat beside him, looping her arm about his shoulder. It was one of those difficult, embarrassed moments that somehow had to be lived through.

Parents looked at one another, bewildered by what was happening. Royce knew the other two fathers and had been introduced to their wives. They weren't from the wrong side of the tracks. They represented solid, respectable families. And yet they were here in Christy's office, brought together by something their boys had done. Royce felt steel bands tighten about his chest, squeezing the breath from him. And he was suddenly faint. He wiped the moisture from his sallow cheeks and groped his way to a chair.

"Believe me," the police chief began, "this is not easy for me and I know it's not easy for any of you."

"What's this all about?" the florid, fat-cheeked father of one of the boys demanded irritably. "Why did you call us down here?"

"And why did you arrest my son?" his wife asked. "What is he supposed to have done?"

"I'm coming to that," Joe said, keeping his voice calm. It was apparent that he had been through this sort of thing many times before with other parents as distraught as these.

One of the boys began to snivel as the officer's gaze rested on him.

"I don't know why you officers don't spend your time going after the real crooks around town," the other father said bitterly. "I don't see why you have to go after good, respectable kids who are just out for a little fun."

Christy peered at him with no visible show of emotion.

"The fun your son and his two friends had wasn't exactly the kind of fun any of us would approve of. They went into Alan Carter's house on the edge of town last night while the Carters were gone and did as thorough a job of wrecking it as I've ever seen."

"Oh, no!" Penny gasped.

The father who had been doing most of the talking continued defensively. "This is a serious charge, Joe. I hope you're prepared to back it up."

For the first time his irritation showed.

"If I wasn't prepared to back it up, Charlie, your son and these other two boys wouldn't be here. One of the neighbors can make a positive identification of all three boys. And, if you'd like to have me do it, I can take fingerprints of the boys and compare them with the prints that are all over the Carter house. There's plenty of evidence to prove that they are guilty."

A mind-deadening numbness took hold of Royce. He couldn't think. He couldn't feel. It was as though he was paralyzed except for sight and hearing. He saw what was taking place. He saw the stern set to Joe's jaw as he carried out the nastiest part of his job; the shock and anger and fear on the faces of the other parents as they became increasingly aware of the full import of what had happened. He saw the terror glittering in the eyes of the three boys.

Joe continued to speak quietly, telling what Craig and his companions had done. How they had broken a window in the Carter home the night before, how they had hacked up the furniture and scrawled obscenties on the walls of the bathroom with black paint. He heard Joe relate how they had broken all the dishes, had cut up the carpet and threw canned food through the plate-glass picture window.

It didn't surprise Royce. It didn't hurt him, at least at that moment. He was impervious to pain.

At last Christy finished. He paused, looking from one to the other.

"Now," he concluded, "the question is, what are we going to do about it?"

"What about Carter?" Royce was surprised to hear his own voice. It had a distant, unnatural ring, as though it wasn't actually his. "Does he plan on pressing charges?"

Christy's gaze met his.

"I don't know about that, Royce."

"Unless I miss my guess," Charlie Bishop put in, "he's going to be a lot more interested in getting his house fixed up than he is in sending three boys to jail."

"You know him, Charlie," his wife said hurriedly, oblivious to the fact that there were others in the room, "and you do a lot of business with him. You'll have to go and see him and get him to refuse to press charges."

Joe Christy broke in testily.

"This is not the time or place to discuss that sort of thing," he told them. "I'm going to release these boys in the custody of you parents. We'll be in touch with you at a later date. OK?"

He got to his feet, signifying that the interview was over.

Craig left the city building between Royce and Penny. He walked in silence, looking from one to the other.

"All right!" he exclaimed bitterly when they were finally in the car. "Why don't you get it over with?"

Royce faced him.

"I wish I knew what to say or do, Craig." He spoke reluctantly, as though it hurt to talk.

"Go ahead! Tell me what a worthless, rotten, no-good son I am! Tell me that I've disgraced all of you and that you wish I'd go away so you'd never have to see me again!"

Hostility and remorse twisted Craig's handsome young face and flamed defiantly in his eyes. His lips quavered and tears clung to his eyelashes, but he held them back forcibly. Since he had been a small boy no one had ever seen him cry. And so it was, even now. The tears were there, but he summoned an inner strength to keep them from rolling down his cheeks.

"Craig!" Penny cried softly. "Don't talk that way! You know how much we love you!"

"I'll bet you do!" His voice choked. "I'll just bet you do!"

She couldn't help it. She started to cry.

Royce said nothing more to Craig until they got home. He hadn't planned on saying anything, even then, but his son called him into the bedroom and closed the door.

"What are you going to do, Dad?" he asked.

"Do?" Royce echoed. "What do you mean, what am I going to do?"

Desperation gripped Craig. "Are you going to let them put me in jail?"

Their eyes met.

"I don't know," Royce replied.

Craig grasped his arm.

"You won't let them send me away, will you?" His grip tightened. "Will you?"

Royce turned thoughtfully and looked into those eyes that were so much like Rita's and the face and delicate coloring of the skin that was so much like hers. She would have expected him to take care of their son, to see that he was properly raised and had every opportunity to become a useful Christian member of society. That was the last thing he was able to do for her. How could he allow the authorities to sentence Craig to a training school or reformatory if it was in his power to stop it?

"I'll have to see what I can do," he said miserably.

"You—you will be able to do something, won't you? After all, Joe Christy's a good friend of yours. You could call him up and talk to him, couldn't you? Or you could get hold of the judge or—or somebody!"

Becky saw that something was wrong and asked her mother about it.

"Did Craig do something bad?" she wanted to know, keeping her voice low so her older brother wouldn't hear her. "Is he in trouble?"

"What makes you think that?" Penny asked.

"Is he?"

Penny put her arm around her serious-faced daughter and drew her close.

"You'll pray for Craig, won't you?"

Becky's eyes were wide and luminous.

"Are they going to put him in jail?"

"What makes you ask that?"

"I heard him and Daddy talking." The tears trickled down her cheeks. "Are they, Mother?"

Penny shook her head. "This is the first time Craig has done something bad. I don't think they'll put him in jail, but we do have to pray for him so he'll be a good boy after this."

"I do pray for him, Mother," Becky assured her. "I pray for him every night."

Later in the evening, when Craig and the other children were in bed, Royce had an opportunity to talk to his wife.

"Do you think it would do any good to talk to Joe about what happened?" he asked. "Do you suppose it might help to get him out of this?"

"It might not hurt."

Agony clouded Royce's eyes. "I just *can't* let them send him to the reformatory."

"They probably wouldn't anyway. It's his first offense."

"You're forgetting the record he's got out at school." He pulled up a chair and sat down across from her, furrows deepening in the space between his eyebrows. "But anyway, I can't take that chance."

Penny folded her magazine nervously and put it aside.

"I don't know why I'm trying to read. I can't even make sense out of it."

Royce picked up a magazine himself, and opened it, but after a moment or two, he put it down.

"Penny," he announced. "I'm going to have to resign my Sunday school class and my job as young people's sponsor and resign from the board of the Children's Bible Time."

She looked up curiously. He had been so thrilled when he had been asked to serve on the board of the interdenominational radio program, and took the duties so seriously.

"Why?" she asked.

Tears filled his eyes.

"How can I help other people's kids when I can't even handle my own?"

Penny got up and sat on the arm of his chair, tangling her fingers in his hair.

"Don't do it yet, Royce," she said softly. "Think about it and pray about it first."

* * *

10

ROYCE WAITED NERVOUSLY in the police chief's office, writhing as miserably in his chair as any lawbreaker waiting to be booked. He didn't like this business of asking special favors; he had heard Joe express contempt of the practice often enough. It went counter to his own conviction about the law and respect for due legal process. But this was different; his own son was involved.

True, Craig and his friends had acted inexcusably. They deserved to be punished for what they had done, but sending them to the reformatory wasn't the answer. There had to be some other way. That was why he was sitting in Joe's office, to see if something could be worked out.

Royce took off his glasses and wiped them carefully with his handkerchief.

There was a noise behind him and he squirmed about to see if it was Joe. Almost gratefully he saw it was a secretary from one of the other offices who came to the door and peeked in, apparently looking for the chief. Or, perhaps she came by to see who was in his office.

Royce's cheeks flamed. He knew Glenville and its propensity for gossip. Every secretary and police officer and janitor in the city building already knew about the vandalism at the Carter home, and who was involved. Before many hours passed, it would be common knowledge around town, including the fact that he had gone to see the chief.

"And do you know who was in to see Joe before nine o'clock in the morning? Royce Lawson was there trying to get his kid out of the jam he's in."

"If it was *my* boy who'd messed up Carter's house they'd have thrown the book at him," some would say, taking vicarious pleasure in the fact that their sons were not involved, as though that elevated their own respectability a notch or two. "But Royce is a friend of Joe's so he can get away with murder!"

"And they call themselves such good Christians!"

Royce did not have to hear the remarks himself to know they were being said. Word would pass from one itching ear to another. He should know; he had heard them often enough. Actually, he had indulged in the same sort of vindictive gossip himself on occasion. He winced as he thought of some of the things he had said about other people, and wished he could take them back.

At the moment, however, he was not concerned about the gossip being spread about himself or Craig. Concern over being talked about would come later, after the shock was gone. After everything was settled he would start to read the contempt in the knowing gaze of those he met and hear tight little whispers behind his back.

"Look at him!" they would say. "As brazen as though he hadn't talked Joe into letting that kid of his get off scot free!"

"He's got a nerve teaching Sunday school and being on the board of that religious radio program for kids!"

"He ought to take care of his own son before he tries to tell anyone else how to live!"

Royce was still sitting near the police chief's desk when his friend's ample frame filled the doorway.

"Hello, Royce."

"Hi." The corners of his mouth turned up in a lifeless,

100

wooden grin, a sham that he had hurriedly tacked in place to hide the agony of his heart.

"I've been expecting you," the chief said. There was no anger or accusation or censure in his voice—only a statement of fact. He closed the door to shut out their voices from the eager ears in the outer office, and advanced to his desk.

"You have?" Surprise edged Royce's voice.

"Yes, I've been expecting you." He sat down and picked up a ball-point pen and fingered it for a time before continuing. "The fathers of the other two boys have already been in to see me."

He expelled his breath slowly. He didn't know why he should draw comfort from that, but he did. At least he wasn't alone in trying to get special favors for his son.

"Then you know why I'm here."

Joe opened a desk drawer and removed a file.

"Bishop and Brown agreed to pay their share of the damages that were done to Alan Carter's house," he said.

"That sounds fair enough."

"Of course that's what Carter is interested in. He doesn't particularly want to see the boys sent to the training school."

At first Royce could not understand exactly what Joe was saying.

"Does that mean there isn't going to be any trial?" he asked.

The police chief lowered his voice.

"It's up to the county attorney, but without a signed complaint he's not going to take action. He's not interested in making a public example of Craig and his friends."

Relief rushed over Royce in a great cleansing wave. There wasn't going to be a prosecution of the boys. Craig wouldn't be running the risk of being sent to the training school and having that stigma on his name. He and Penny wouldn't have to face the shame of having a son with a record.

"I—I don't know what to say, Joe. I don't know how to thank you."

His friend's gaze was even.

"It's nothing I have done, Royce," he said. "I'd be powerless to help in a situation like this."

Royce flushed. He hadn't intended the implication that his remark indicated. He wanted to apologize for it, but he knew it would only increase the embarrassment of the moment.

Although the general agreement had been worked out, there was one more ordeal for Royce and Penny to go through. They had to meet with the parents of the other boys in the county attorney's office to work out the terms of settlement with Alan Carter. The only stipulation the county attorney insisted upon was that he be permitted to call the boys in and talk with them before informing them of the decision that had been reached

"My chief concern," he explained, "is that the boys don't get the idea that because their parents are respected members of the community they can get away with anything. They've got to be impressed with the seriousness of what they have done and to understand how serious another infraction of the law would be."

"You're not going to have to worry about my son anymore," Bishop boasted. "I gave him a good hiding last night. He knows better than to get into trouble again."

Royce and Penny were careful not to tell Craig what had been decided in the meeting with the county attorney, but news of the decision not to press charges got home to Craig almost as soon as they did. One of the other set of parents relayed the good news to their son and he called his buddies.

Craig was sprawled on the divan when they came in, hands cupped behind his head and a triumphant grin tugging at one corner of his thin mouth. Royce noticed the change in him at once.

"Well, I see you got back, Dad."

Royce's head bobbed curtly.

"Yes, we're back."

"I didn't think it would be so bad."

Royce spun on his heel, anger smoking in his distraught face.

"Just what did you mean by that?"

Royce's sudden show of temper seemed to startle Craig. He sat up quickly, the smile leaving his face.

"You don't need to get so shook up about it. I was just talking about what happened in the county attorney's office, that's all."

Royce went into the bedroom and slipped out of his coat. He didn't know why he was so disturbed at Craig's show of relief. He felt the same way. It was as though the weight of the world had been taken off his back.

But, what about his son? The nagging doubt persisted that it had been too easy for Craig. Actually, the episode had cost Craig nothing at all. Nothing had happened to him to make him aware of the fact that breaking the law didn't pay. Yet, what could Royce have done differently? He couldn't let them send his son away.

Craig didn't have much to say the rest of the afternoon except when somebody talked with him. He didn't tease Becky and was even nice to the twins. And, as soon as dinner was over, he went to his room to study.

"Did you notice how nice Craig was tonight?" Becky whispered to her mother as they did the dishes.

"He was real sweet," Penny acknowledged.

"I just know he's going to change." She thought about that for a time. "I've been praying for him every night."

"So have Daddy and I."

Royce, however, was not so sure that everything was going to be all right.

"I hope so, Penny," he told her when they were alone for the night. "I sincerely hope so. But it's such a serious thing. We can't afford to make any mistakes."

She sat quite still, hands folded in her lap. She understood how Royce felt. The same gnawing doubts chewed at the corners of her own mind. She was thinking of his belligerence and the times he had deceived them.

"Do you remember the ad for that Christian military academy I was showing you last week?"

"It's in Oklahoma, isn't it?"

"What would you think about sending Craig there?"

Hurt flecked her usually merry eyes.

"But he'd be so far from home, Royce. I wouldn't like that part of it."

"I wouldn't like that either." He leaned forward earnestly. "But we're at the crossroads with Craig right now, Penny. What we do in the next few months may decide what the rest of his life is going to be. We don't dare make a mistake."

She did not reply immediately. What Royce said was true. They had to get hold of Craig now, while he was still young and pliable enough to be changed. It was like the principal said, the Glenville school wasn't able to give him the sort of supervision and discipline he needed. And she and Royce didn't seem to be able to give it either. At least Craig wouldn't accept it from them. A military school with solid Christian training might be the answer. But to think that he would be taken out of their home and they wouldn't be able to see him for months seemed unbearable.

"It'll be terribly expensive, won't it?" she asked. There was a hopeful tinge to her voice.

"That's one big drawback — it will be terribly expensive. Schools like that always are. We'd probably have to borrow the money."

He hesitated. They had been having enough financial problems without the additional burden of a private school. He didn't know quite how they could manage any other large expenditures; but if it would do what had to be done for Craig, it would be worth whatever sacrifices they had to make.

Penny's gaze sought his.

"You know I'm with you, Royce, in whatever you decide to do."

He half expected Craig to protest bitterly at being sent away to a military school. They had asked him to do few things in the past two years that he had done willingly. However, he surprised them both by raising no objections.

"I suppose it wouldn't be so bad. When would I go?"

"I don't know." Royce reached for the phone. "We'll have to see if they'll take you first."

The school agreed to take him whenever Royce could get him there.

"Fine. We'll leave the first thing in the morning."

Craig nodded his approval.

"I want to get out of this stupid town before everybody finds out about us and what we did," he muttered, scowling darkly. "I don't want to have everybody I know talking about me."

Royce did not reply, but he knew exactly how Craig felt. He felt the same. He was ashamed to admit it, but he had crossed the street in the middle of the block that very morning to keep from meeting a friend he had known since he first moved to Glenville. Now that this story was breaking, he wished he could get so far from Glenville no one would ever have heard of the place.

It was a grubby, gossiping little town. He didn't blame Craig for wanting to get away from it.

They got Aunt Sally to come and stay with the three younger children while they took Craig to Oklahoma. He acted as though it didn't matter to him that he was going to be away from home, but Penny cried half the way home. At first Royce tried to quiet her. But when that was unsuccessful, he let her sob until she could cry no more.

"It's for his own good," he reminded her when she was quiet.

"I know," she said, wiping at her eyes, "but right now that doesn't help a great deal."

That night in the motel they decided what to tell people who asked why they took their son out of the public high school.

"Actually, it isn't anybody's business except ours. I don't see why we have to tell them anything."

"I know," Penny answered. "But I also know Glenville. The people at home will make it their business. They always do."

The corners of his mouth twitched and anger spotted his cheeks with crimson.

Glenville was arrogant in its demand to know everything.

Every painful secret detail had to be brought out into the open, examined critically and elaborated on. What they did not know, they surmised and speculated, always imagining the worst, always enlarging on the facts on the "iceburg theorem" that for every detail of a story that was out to the public there were at least ten worse items that were hidden from view.

"What will we tell them?" Penny asked again.

"We'll simply say that Craig's been a bit hard to handle," Royce replied, working out the statement as he went along. "And that his grades haven't been too good. We'll tell them he'll be made to study and get a little better education at the military academy." He paused. "And, that's the truth."

"As far as it goes."

"They've already been talking," he retorted, anger flecking his voice. "They won't believe what we tell them, anyway."

She wasn't entirely satisfied with that story, because although it was the truth, it was also quite close to lying. Yet she had to admit that Royce was right in his reasoning. It really wasn't anybody's business why Craig was in Oklahoma.

Royce had been right about the gossip. It flamed like a range fire in the community and swept on the wind of self-righteousness and pious indignation through every level of society. Royce was confronted with it in the post office and on the street. Most preferred to talk behind his back, but there were those, more bold than the rest, who faced him with it.

"Now I'll tell you where you made your biggest mistake," one graying individual informed him knowingly. "You should've made that kid of yours stay and take his medicine. That's the only way. If you want to get him straightened out, I'll tell you what you've got to do. Get him back here in Glenville. Make him walk down the streets of this town and look people in the eyes. He'll soon find out what everybody thinks of the likes of him. He'll find out he's got to live right or nobody will have anything to do with him."

After the man left, Royce could not remember what he had

106

answered in reply, but he realized that what he said would not have mattered to the self-styled expert who came in to give them the benefit of his own wisdom and years of experience. His caller had come to give advice, to set things right; he had not come to listen.

There were others who had different ideas, but were just as loud and dogmatic in their assertions.

"The trouble is that you've been too lax with Craig," he was told. "Now, when our kids were growing up we knew where they were and what they were doing all the time. And if they didn't do what I told them to they knew they were going to catch it from me. I had 'em all out to the woodshed more'n once. It takes discipline to raise kids right."

Royce's visitor leaned back in the chair and crossed his legs. Pride pushed his face into a broad smile and gleamed in his eyes.

A business acquaintance found still another reason for what had happened with Craig. He came into the architect's office just to tell him about it.

"I always hate to see kids get into trouble," he began, "especially good kids like Craig."

Royce laid his T square aside and looked up, waiting. That was the way most people began. They hated to see good kids get into trouble, but — and then the advice would come. Everybody knew where he and Penny had failed. Everybody knew what they should have done. The frown lines about his mouth deepened and his face grew somber.

"Yes." His irritation showed. "It's bad when anyone gets into trouble."

"Y'know, Royce, I hate to tell you this because I like you and that wife of yours. Always have." He hitched up a chair and dropped into it, squinting waspishly at Royce. "But, you're too religious, both of you. That's what's been wrong. You've pushed religion down that kid's throat so much he just naturally resents it. Now, take me and my wife. We consider ourselves good Christian people, but we never made our kids go to Sunday school or church in their whole lives unless they wanted to. And they didn't turn out so bad."

107

Royce remained silent.

"It was all that religion you forced on him that made Craig do what he did."

"Oh?" His voice was mild. "How about the Bishop boy who was in this thing with Craig? To my knowledge they've never had him in Sunday school or church at all. Would you say he's too religious too?"

The muscles in the caller's face tightened.

"You don't need to get so huffy about it. I was just trying to help."

11

AFTER A COUPLE OF WEEKS the gossip about Craig began to slacken, but it didn't seem so to Royce. True, people no longer mentioned it to him, but he was sure he still read scorn in their eyes as he met them on the street. He was sure the talk just went underground, that the town was still talking about him and his wayward son.

For several weeks he didn't want to go anywhere or visit with anyone. Even when he had to go into the bank or one of the stores, he transacted his business as quickly as possible and hurried out. Only his relationship with the church did not change — they still attended with the same regularity. He was a little more withdrawn and less inclined to speak out during business meetings, but they were there, doing what they could.

Once or twice he told Penny he was thinking about resigning from the board of the Children's Bible Hour, but since he had said nothing about it for a time, she supposed he had forgotten about it. Such was not the case, however.

"I've got to resign, Penny," he informed her one evening, a month or so after they had taken Craig to Oklahoma. "I can't be of help to them now. I'm only bringing shame and discredit to them."

"What makes you say that?"

His gaze came up to meet hers, the hurt burning in his eyes.

"Haven't you read those verses in the Bible about serving God?" he asked. "Christian men are supposed to have their own families under subjection before assuming positions of responsibility in God's work. And I sure can't claim to have done that."

Penny knew the verses he was talking about. He had read them to her a number of times since they began having problems with Craig. There had been other times when he was going to stop everything he was doing in the church.

"But this is different," she protested, thinking to talk him out of it once more. "You've tried to handle Craig; it isn't your fault he's like he is."

"The only thing different about it is that it happens to be me and our boy instead of someone else. That's all."

In bed that night, their arms wrapped about each other, they discussed the matter at length. Penny used every argument she could command, but it was useless. Royce had reached his decision. The following morning he called Dr. Benson, the director of the radio program, and made an appointment for him and Penny to see him in Omaha the first of the week.

Dr. Benson must have sensed the problem. He had asked his wife to join them for lunch in a secluded little restaurant where they could talk without interruption.

"Now," he said when they had ordered and the waitress was gone, "what is this problem you wanted to talk over?"

Royce hesitated, staring at his plate. It wasn't easy to tell someone like Dr. Benson the whole sordid story about Craig. It wasn't easy to tell a man like him that he wasn't worthy of serving on his board. But it had to be done, it was the only honorable way.

Royce began slowly, forcing out the words. Dr. Benson already knew about Rita's death and his remarriage to

Penny. And Royce had told him about Craig and mentioned the problems Martha Laird had caused. Starting with Craig's resentment of the twins and his apparent dislike of Sunday school and church, he traced his son's troubles at school and finally the vandalism which caused them to send him to Oklahoma to finish his high school education.

Dr. Benson and his wife nodded understandingly.

"So," he concluded, "I've come to tell you that I'm going to resign as a member of your board."

The director of the radio program reached in his pocket with stubby fingers and drew out his worn Testament.

"I know exactly how you feel, but did you know that God has a promise for you regarding Craig?"

He shook his head numbly. He had tried to find help and encouragement from the Bible at different times. There were a few verses he tried to claim, but they had become so meaningless he couldn't even remember them.

Dr. Benson flipped the pages to Acts 16:31. "Believe on the Lord Jesus Christ, and thou shalt be saved, and thy house," he read. "That's a conditional promise."

Royce had read that verse many times. He could have quoted it from memory. But he had never thought of it as a promise concerning Craig, let alone as a conditional proise.

"I'm going to ask both of you a few questions. Have you lived a consistent Christian life before your son?"

Royce's forehead crinkled. They probably hadn't; at the moment all he could recall were his own shortcomings. Yet, they tried to live consistent Christian lives. Their failures were not because of faulty desire. They had even changed churches in order to get sound teaching for their children.

Those things he told Dr. Benson.

"Have you prayed for Craig regularly?"

Had they prayed for him? Was there ever a moment when they were not praying for him? Royce remembered all those hours when he and Penny had been on their knees pleading with God to make their son what he ought to have been.

"Have you ever talked with him about his personal re-

111

sponsibility to the Lord Jesus Christ? Have you told him how to be saved?"

He had talked with him so often that Craig used it as an excuse for turning his back on God. "I might not hate to go to church so much if you hadn't preached to me all the time," his son used to say.

He acknowledged that he and Penny had tried to do all of those things.

"But we probably failed miserably."

"We all fail," Mrs. Benson put in gently. "But I'm sure God looks in our hearts and sees what we are trying to do."

"Exactly," Dr. Benson went on. "He counts our motives for righteousness just as He counts our faith for righteousness."

This was something Royce had never considered. It changed everything, giving him new hope and encouragement. If God counted his motives for righteousness, then He would undertake for Craig regardless of the mistakes Royce and Penny made. No longer would the full burden be upon them. No longer would they be forced to weigh each decision with the knowledge that the wrong choice, an error in judgment on their part, could keep Craig from yielding his heart and his life to Christ.

"Then we should thank God for His promise to bring Craig to a personal commitment to Jesus Christ as Saviour and Lord," the radio minister said.

He went on to tell Royce that no good could come by his resignation from the board.

"There are always attacks of Satan on those who try to serve Christ," he explained. "And one of his favorite targets is our children. If you resign, Royce, you will be giving Satan the victory over this area of your life."

Royce was not easily convinced, but finally he understood what Dr. Benson was saying, and agreed to stay on.

"We'll be praying for all three of you," Mrs. Benson told Penny quietly, extending her hand.

Penny's eyes were translucent with tears as they parted.

Royce had other periods of dejection, but never again

did he feel that he should stop working in the church or the other Christian organizations he was interested in.

* * *

Craig seemed to like the military academy in Oklahoma. He wrote home about it often, going into detail about the athletic events. That was a new interest for him in spite of his size. The coach had taken one look at him and told him he was going out for football.

"There's not much else to do around here, so I checked out a suit," he wrote. "To tell you the truth, it's sort of fun."

Becky's eyes sparkled as she heard Penny read the letter aloud.

"I hope the people in Glenville find out what a fine football player Craig is," she said loyally. "Then they'd be sorry they said such terrible things about him."

It wasn't long until the town did learn about Craig's exploits. The school's publicity department fed news items about him to the *Glenville Gazette*. Royce clipped them all and pasted them in a scrapbook. Like Becky he was more pleased than he would admit when there was a story about Craig in the local paper and someone would stop him on the street to mention it.

"I wish that boy of yours was still going to school here. We could use him in that backfield of ours."

"I'm just as glad he's where he is."

In the intervening months he had become a strong critic of public schools and an ardent advocate of private schools.

"The big classes we've got here in Glenville just about eliminate the chance for personal development," Royce would boast. "They're all right for the average kid, but they're not geared for the exceptional student. I'd like nothing better than to be able to send all of my kids to private schools for their high school work."

Although he would never have admitted it to anyone else, he talked often with Penny about the effect military discipline would have on Craig.

"It scares me when I think of the way he would have turned out if we'd tried to keep him in school here. I'm sure

113

he would have gotten himself into a real jam before he graduated, but now I don't have a single worry about him. The discipline he's getting is exactly what he needs, it's going to make a man of him."

Penny wished she had the confidence in the school and what they were doing for Craig that Royce had. It was true that they had been able to handle him. At least the school authorities hadn't written them of any trouble they were having with him, and from his letters it didn't sound as though his activities were being restricted because of disciplinary measures. Yet, there was something that disturbed her.

For a while she remained silent, but finally she voiced her fears to Royce.

"Neither Craig nor the school authorities have written us anything regarding his spiritual life, and that's the thing we've been the most concerned about."

Royce had somehow assumed that because Craig seemed to be getting along well at the school he was probably progressing spiritually. But now that Penny asked the question he had to find out for sure.

"I'll call the chaplain at the school tomorrow," he said, "and see what I can find out."

Craig was doing quite well in his studies, the chaplain told Royce. He was doing B work in two subjects and C in the rest. That wasn't bad for a fellow whose average had been D- in his home school.

"As to his spiritual condition, I really couldn't say," the chaplain said. "I've had several talks with him, and he does know what Christianity is all about, but I'm not sure of his personal relationship with Christ."

Penny was even more disturbed than she had been before, but Royce was remarkably complacent.

"We can't expect everything at once," he said. "Let's be thankful he's in a place where there are concerned men working with him. He'll come around before he graduates; you wait and see. The teachers there know exactly how to handle fellows like him; they're *trained*."

While the letters Craig wrote home were reassuring to his parents, those he sent to his former schoolmates were written with a different pen. A close friend of Penny's talked with her about it.

"Our son, Dick, had a letter from Craig last week," she said.

Penny looked up. Something about Edna's tone was disturbing, as though she didn't want to talk about the letter but felt compelled to.

"Yes?"

"I don't want to be gossiping or to tell things that I shouldn't," she went on, obviously embarrassed. "But Dick let me read it and—and I thought you should know what it said. I'd want to know if he were my son."

"If it's something we should know about, we'll be very grateful to you for telling us."

Edna cleared her throat and leaned closer, lowering her voice so Becky and the twins could not hear her guarded whispers.

"It told about a big drinking party the fellows went on— and Craig said he was one of them. He was boasting about how much he drank and how drunk they all were."

Edna's whispered message chilled Penny like the frigid blast of wind off polar ice. This was something she had never seriously considered might happen. She could see Craig getting into mischief; she could even see him doing acts of vandalism. But drinking was something else! She and Royce had been so careful to warn Craig about the evils of alcohol.

She dreaded having to tell Royce about it. She wished she didn't have to tell him, but she knew—even as the thought came—that she had to. They didn't keep anything from each other.

He surprised her by not being more disturbed than he was. He laid aside the paper, but his expression did not change. Momentarily his lack of concern was irritating.

"Edna isn't a gossip," she repeated, "and she didn't tell

me about it because she wants to make us feel bad or cause trouble for Craig."

"I'm sure of that." He realized then that she was upset, and he laid a hand on her arm reassuringly. "But it doesn't particularly bother me."

Perplexity frowned at Royce from Penny's calm blue eyes.

"That surprises me. I thought you'd be as disturbed as I am about it."

"I would be," he acknowledged, 'if I had even the most remote idea that it could be true. But you know how Craig has always been about impressing people, and especially his friends."

Penny's gaze shifted uneasily to Royce's face.

"But the letter sounded so true—so genuine."

"Oh, he'd make it sound good. He always does."

Craig had always been careless about telling the truth if something else suited his purpose, Penny had to admit. And he was cunning enough with his falsehoods to deceive anyone he wanted to. Yet the letter had the firm, clear ring of truth in it. That thought seared a white-hot mark across her mind.

"What if it is true?" she asked. "Don't you think we ought to get in touch with the school authorities so they can check it out?"

He squinted narrowly across the table at her.

"I'm not that concerned, Penny. I'm convinced he's only trying to make an impression on his buddies. A telephone call from us might get him in trouble with the authorities."

She hesitated thoughtfully. "I suppose you're right."

"We've entrusted Craig to the people at the school," he continued. "The entire staff is well trained to handle boys, so let's put our trust in them and let them take care of him. They'll manage."

Penny could not put the matter entirely aside. The next morning after the twins were off to school, she wrote Craig a long letter, reminding him once again of the dangers of drinking and expressing the hope that he would never start.

116

She didn't know whether it did any good or not, but once it was mailed she felt better.

By the end of the year, Craig was maintaining a B average and Royce and Penny received a note of commendation from the principal on the work their son had been doing since he had come to the academy.

A smile shone from the lines about Royce's mouth.

"It's been tough to pay the bills to keep him there, but I guess this shows that we did the right thing."

"I'm so proud of him."

"So am I." Royce paced across the living room, his fingers still tightly closed about the letter. "You know, Penny, I'd like to post this note and Craig's grades on the bulletin board at church so some of our *friends* could see it. I'd like to have everybody in town know the kind of school work he's doing now."

The following year was a repetition of the first. His grades slipped slightly at the close of the term's first nine weeks, but after that they climbed back to a respectable B average. He earned a place at tackle on the starting team during the football season and established an acceptable record wrestling in the heavyweight division during the winter and spring.

Royce had almost forgotten what it was like to worry about Craig. They looked forward to getting his letters and he seemed to look forward to theirs.

They found it increasingly difficult to meet the added expenses of the military academy and to keep their own bills current. Twice Royce had to go to the bank and borrow money. Not that he minded it or the pinch the private school put on the activities of the rest of the family. Even the other kids understood.

"I don't care if I don't get a new bike this year," Becky said. "I want Craig to be able to stay in school."

Royce's eyes filled suddenly and he wrapped an arm about his only daughter and drew her close to him.

"Now don't you worry about Craig being able to stay in school," he told her. "We'll manage that too. You've been long enough without a bike."

That night he had her new bicycle in the trunk of the car. He didn't tell her that they had to pay it off by the month.

When Craig came back to Glenville at the close of his second year at the military academy he talked with his parents about coming back home for his senior year.

Royce could not hide his own disappointment. "I thought you liked it at the school in Oklahoma."

"I do, but I'd like to graduate with my friends. Besides, a fellow gets sort of lonesome so far away from home."

Becky sidled up to his chair and wriggled into the crook of his arm.

"It gets lonesome without you too," she told him. "It gets awful lonesome."

They talked it over and somewhat reluctantly agreed that he could stay in Glenville for his senior year.

12

ALTHOUGH ROYCE AND PENNY had serious doubts about the wisdom of allowing Craig to come back to Glenville to finish high school, he seemed to get along quite well. He studied at home with some degree of regularity and was concerned about his grades. Not as much as some of the better students, Royce had to acknowledge, but his attitude was far different than it had been. He was disturbed about the fact that his B average had slipped to a C and went to talk to his teachers about it.

"I'd never dare tell Craig this," Royce said to Penny, "but it would have been a minor miracle if he could do B work here. In Oklahoma he was forced to study every night; they made him do his best. Here, he's on his own."

Penny nodded without enthusiasm.

"We've got to look at the grades he was getting before he went away to school."

She had to admit that Craig was doing better in many ways. He hadn't been called into the principal's office since the school term started, as far as they knew. And he was more agreeable to be around. But she was still vaguely disturbed about him in ways she could not quite understand.

He still treated her as though she was a broken-down piece of furniture he would have discarded if he could. He didn't speak to her unless he had to. In speaking of her she was "she" or "her" instead of "Mother." When he wanted to talk with Royce, which was often, he got him into a bedroom alone, lowering his voice to a whisper. Usually he attempted to swear his dad to secrecy before talking to him. Recognizing that Craig only wanted to hurt Penny, Royce refused to go along with him, but that didn't stop Craig from trying.

Craig didn't go out often at night; but when he did, it was with boys Penny did not like or trust. They would stride arrogantly into the house, drop into the best chairs as though they owned them, or switch channels on television to something they happened to like better, regardless of whether Becky or the twins were watching. Royce and Penny had to talk with them several times about it.

Becky's dislike of Craig's new friends smoldered, but she said nothing against them. She was too loyal to her brother for that, but it was obvious that she didn't like them any better than her mother did.

Penny mentioned her attitude to Royce.

"Come now," he chided. "You can't take one kid's appraisal of another and make it mean anything. I can't say that I'm so crazy about Craig's friends either, but Becky not liking them probably doesn't mean any more than the fact that she doesn't like their looks."

She was not convinced.

"Have you forgotten how it was when we were kids?" she asked. "We knew which kids at school were living decent lives and which ones weren't, even though the teaching staff and most of the adults in town were fooled."

"You may be right." But he still was not willing to admit that she was.

He was in complete agreement with Penny, however, that Craig had made no marked improvement spiritually. He still slouched at the table during Bible reading and prayer, the muscles in his jaw drawing into ugly knots and a sneer tugging at his mouth. The rest of the family took turns reading and praying, but not Craig. He seemed to draw a certain amount of pleasure from refusing to take part until finally Royce no longer asked him. Their family devotions were conducted as though he wasn't there.

Craig would go to church occasionally if Royce pounced on him hard enough, but it was obvious to everyone that he was there only because he had to be. He would scoot down in the seat with his knees on the pew in front of him until they were higher than his head. There he would sit, oblivious to the service that was being conducted. The congregation stood and were seated. They sang and prayed and passed the collection plate, but he made no effort to move, let alone take part. Before the service was over, half the people close by were watching him, a situation that he greatly enjoyed.

He refused to go to Sunday school or the youth meetings.

"That old junk?" he would echo. "You won't catch me there."

Royce was most concerned about it.

"Just what is your relationship with Christ, Craig?" he would ask.

His son unhinged his gangling frame and sat up, scorn mounting his cool smile.

"Now what would you say it was, Dad?"

Royce didn't know why, but Craig's irritable manner placed him on the defensive. "The only way you can be truly happy is to walk with God."

"For cryin' out loud!" He acted as though he would have enjoyed using stronger language. "Don't you *ever* get tired of preaching at me? Ever since I can remember you've tried to stuff religion down my throat. I'm sick of it!"

Royce's eyebrows drew together. "It must not've done much good for me to preach at you!" he exploded. "You're still living the way you please." He was sorry for what he said the instant the words escaped his lips, but there was no changing them now—no calling them back. He would have apologized to Craig and asked his forgiveness, but

Craig wouldn't listen to that either. He only heard what he wanted to hear.

"Why don't you live your life, Dad, and let me live mine?" he asked. "I'm satisfied with myself just the way I am."

Penny talked with Royce about preaching at Craig so much.

"I'm afraid we'll only drive him farther away if we keep talking to him about it," she said.

He wiped his forehead with a moist hand.

"I suppose you're right," he admitted, "but when I think about Craig and his attitude toward Christ I get so upset I hardly know what I'm doing."

"I know." Penny tenderly slipped her hand into his, knowing what he was trying to explain to her. She, too, had experienced the same frustration, the same confusion and bewilderment. "I know."

"I feel so helpless."

She looked away quickly to keep him from seeing the sparkle of tears in her eyes. She had to be strong for his sake and had to maintain control of herself.

Penny couldn't understand Royce and the way anything connected with Craig affected him. She had always thought of her husband as a strong personality—a person who was sure of what he wanted and how to get it. When he decided that he was taking his family out of their former church, he was unmoved by the committee that came to dissuade him, and he took the criticism that followed his action without wavering.

But when anything came up about Craig, he was weak and uncertain, as though afraid someone had stolen his reason. It bothered Penny more than she liked to admit. It also bothered her that Craig knew and capitalized on his dad's weakness.

"You aren't going to let him have the car tonight, are you?" she would whisper to Royce.

"After the time he got in last Saturday night? I should say not!"

Occasionally he stood firm, but usually Craig would get the car in spite of Royce's fervent denials.

Usually Penny didn't say anything about it, but there were times when she could not keep quiet.

"I know I said I wasn't going to let him use the car tonight, but he promised to be in early and not to leave the city limits."

"He promised the last time and you remember that Ed McIntosh said he saw him in Hamilton. That's a hundred miles away."

Royce did not reply. What could he say? Everything Penny said was true. He recognized his own weakness as far as Craig was concerned and tried to do something about it, but somehow he could not be consistent. After a brief attempt to bring their oldest son in line, he would begin to make exceptions until the situation was soon the same as ever.

In the spring, Craig graduated from high school and got a job with the local livestock commission company helping with their weekly cattle and hog sales. Royce actually hadn't expected him to stay there long. Craig didn't know anything about cattle and hogs and had never shown any particular interest in them. The only times he had ever been around livestock of any kind was when he went out to the farm with Royce on Saturday afternoons to go horseback riding. But it was soon apparent that he had a natural bent for judging livestock. Even farmers who spent their lives around stock admired his shrewdness. It wasn't long until his employer was letting him buy a few cattle if he thought some money could be made on them. In spite of his age, he did well enough to warrant continuing the practice.

Royce was glad to see Craig working at a job he enjoyed, but secretly he was disappointed. He had wanted him to become an architect and come back to Glenville after he finished his education and go into business with him. Even when Craig was small, Royce had that dream, but he had said nothing to anyone except Penny about it.

"That would be nice," she said, knowing how much he

123

was counting on it, "if it's what Craig wants. But we shouldn't plan too strongly on it. We can't live his life for him."

"I know." A wistful glint shone in his eyes. "And I wouldn't want him to come in unless he really wants to. But I don't think it would be wrong for me to pray for that, do you?"

He hadn't asked her about it, but he was sure that she was praying about the matter too.

It wasn't only that Royce wanted Craig to become an architect. Even if he didn't come in with him he wanted him to get a college education. At different times when the opportunity presented itself, he talked about the advantages of going on to college.

"Not me," his son retorted. "I can get along very well without that. I've had all the school I need to last the rest of my life."

And that was the end of the matter. Royce knew it would be useless to continue talking with Craig, but he sent for some college catalogs and left them lying around in the hope that they would spark interest in Craig. There was never any evidence, however, that he even looked at them. If he did, he was careful to put them back exactly as he found them.

That fall he started going with a girl who came in from the country to work. She was a year older than he was and was almost as tall—a statuesque brunette with a warm smile and scintillating eyes the color of her hair. Royce and Penny didn't meet Dianne Whitfield immediately, but they heard a lot about her.

"She's from a lovely family," Penny was told. "And she's charming."

"Craig always has had good taste."

Her friend's eyes narrowed. "I just hope he's good enough for her," she retorted acidly.

Penny winced. She knew what Mable meant, but that didn't make it any easier.

The change that came over Craig was marked. He had never shown any particular interest in girls until he began to date Dianne. He had dated several during high school, but there had never been one who meant more to him than another. Now, however, he took Dianne out once or twice a week. He bought himself a new suit and some white shirts and ties, items he hadn't bought since he started getting his own clothes.

He laughed and joked around the house and, on occasion, even talked with the twins without teasing or growling at them.

"I don't know that girl," Royce said to Penny, "but we certainly owe her a debt of gratitude for the change she's working in Craig."

They were delighted when he wanted to bring her over to meet them.

"You've never met any girl like her, Dad. She's great."

"Would you like to have her over for dinner Sunday?" Penny asked.

"Could we?" Craig's eyes gleamed.

"Why don't you ask her to be ready a little early so she can go to church with us?" Royce said.

Craig's smile faded and scorn darkened his face.

"Ask her to go to church with us?" he echoed. "For cryin' out loud! Don't you *ever* think about anything except going to church?"

Royce stiffened.

"I'm sorry I even mentioned it."

"You should be."

He didn't know why he kept pushing Craig about things like going to church and reading his Bible. It had never done any good. Yet, he couldn't resist. And when Craig snarled back at him he was angry and indignant.

The following Sunday Dianne Whitfield came for dinner. Craig proudly brought her into the house and introduced her to his family.

"This is Dianne." His lips caressed the name.

The tall young lady at his side took half a step forward in a quick, friendly gesture and extended her hand. She was even prettier than Royce had expected, a gay, vivacious girl with a smile like the window to a happy heart. There was a gentleness in her eyes.

"I'm so glad to know you."

"We're delighted to know you, too, my dear."

Craig scowled his disapproval at Penny for her remark. It was obvious that he wanted them to be friendly, but not too friendly. Penny scarcely noticed that he didn't approve. She liked this regal young lady their son had brought home. There was a sweetness and warmth about her that revealed much about her character. She talked easily about her family and seemed to like the twins and Becky.

And, she was aware of the amount of work involved in getting a Sunday dinner. Although Penny protested that there was nothing she could do to help, she was soon in the kitchen cutting celery and carrots.

Craig, who had been watching the proceedings in the kitchen with growing dismay, turned to his dad.

"I don't know why *she* had to get Dianne out in the kitchen. What's Dianne going to think, being in the house five minutes and being put to work?"

"As I recall," Royce said, "she was the one who suggested that she help Mother."

"Well, I don't like it."

He was still frowning his disapproval when Penny called them to dinner. As soon as they finished eating he insisted on leaving.

"But I should help your mother with the dishes," Dianne protested.

"Becky can help with the dishes. She always does. I've got some things I've got to do this afternoon."

She pushed back from the table. "It will only take a few minutes."

Craig's voice tightened. "Are you going with me, or aren't you?"

Dianne's cheeks flushed as she got her coat. "I'm awfully sorry, Mrs. Lawson."

"We've got to run." Craig almost pushed her out the door ahead of him.

126

Becky went to the window and watched until they were in the car driving away.

"Isn't she nice?"

"She's a lovely girl," Penny said.

"Are they going to get married, Mom?" one of the twins wanted to know. "Are they?"

Royce did not voice his opinion of Dianne, but he approved of her very much. She wasn't silly like so many girls her age and she came from a good family. She could be good for Craig. In fact, it seemed to him that Craig was already showing evidence of Dianne's good influence.

At first he was with Dianne once or twice a week, but it wasn't long until he was seeing her twice as often. Every week or so he brought her home with him for a meal or to watch television. It seemed as though he was anxious to have her get better acquainted with his parents. They were pleased about that. He had never wanted them to know his friends before, and he hadn't voluntarily spent many evenings at home the past several years.

Then Craig and Dianne had a disagreement and broke up for a time. Royce never did learn what they fought about, but he figured it must have been caused by Craig's unreasonable jealousy. At any rate, they didn't go together for several weeks.

Craig refused to talk about it at home.

"It's nothing!" he snapped. "Nothing at all."

That night he didn't come home until after three. Royce was awake when he came stumbling in. The next night he didn't come home at all. Royce knew that too; he had lain awake half the night listening for him and worrying. When Craig finally drove up, it was morning and the rest of the family was eating breakfast. He tried to slip in without being seen, but his dad heard him and met him at the door.

"We've been worried about you."

His son's bloodshot eyes narrowed defensively. "I'm a big boy now," he slurred. "I can take care of myself."

Royce tried to ignore the sickly sweet smell of liquor that Craig wore like cologne.

He had known, then, that trouble was coming. It had become a constant dread with him in the days that followed. Now that dread had become reality. Craig had been arrested for drunken driving and stealing a car.

Royce and Penny went down to the police station as early as possible the next morning and Joe Christy had one of the officers go down to the cellblock to get him. Royce would never forget how Craig stood ramrod straight, eyes blazing his defiance until the officer went out. Nor could he forget how the sham and pretence dropped away with the closing of the door. Craig became a little boy again, coming forward eagerly and grasping Royce's coat lapels.

"You aren't going to let them do anything to me, are you, Dad?" he demanded, his voice shrill. "Are you?"

It was all Royce could do to speak.

"This is a serious charge, Craig."

"Don't you think I know that? I'm the one who's been locked up. Remember?"

Royce eyed his son miserably. Was this the baby Rita died bringing into the world? Was this his son?

"Joe Christy's a friend of yours. He won't do anything if you talk to him." Desperation sharpened his thin, rasping voice.

"There's nothing I can do this time."

Craig's despair grew. "You could go see the people at Acme Motors," he shrilled. "They got their car back and it hadn't been wrecked or anything. It didn't hurt them any."

Royce's gaze mirrored his own hopelessness.

"If you go and talk to them, Dad, they won't do anything. They'll refuse to prosecute."

Craig was still pleading with him when the time was up and he had to go back to his cell.

"You see them, Dad!" he called over his shoulder. "Go and talk to them right away."

Numbly Royce guided Penny out of the city building to their car. The sun was gently warming the day, but he was bleak and cold within. For him it seemed that the sun would never shine again.

They met an old friend on the sidewalk who smiled and spoke to them.

"Royce," Penny chided softly. "You didn't speak to Wally."

He jerked himself erect.

"What?"

"You didn't speak to Wally Evers."

He eyed her blankly. "Where was he?"

13

ROYCE DIDN'T GO TO WORK that morning. He sat bleakly in the living room, gaze fixed on the cold fireplace. Penny came and sat beside him.

"What are we going to do?" she asked.

He raised his head and pivoted to stare at her.

"What can we do?"

She hesitated, caught in her own misery.

"Do you think they'll put him in the reformatory?" she asked at last, giving voice to the question that tormented them both.

He got to his feet and stared down at her, almost as though she was a stranger.

"I could never stand that," he mumbled.

"Neither could I."

He waited for the last sound of the striking clock to die.

"I know Craig hasn't done right, but it isn't going to help to put him in the reformatory. That would only make matters worse."

That afternoon he went down to see the county attorney. Disgust gleamed in the attorney's eyes. He didn't like it that Royce had come to see him, but he was cordial and suggested a meeting with Craig, the authorities and the owner of Acme Motors.

After that meeting the attorney talked with Craig alone for an hour or more while Royce waited in the outer office. Then he was called in.

The attorney was reading Craig's first statement to the police when he entered and sat down.

"There's no doubt in my mind but that Craig is emotionally disturbed," he said, looking up. "It's my considered opinion that he should see a psychiatrist."

Royce and Penny had talked about that very thing the night before. Neither of them knew much about psychiatry, but they were sure there was something wrong with their oldest son. He acted different than the other kids in the family, sullen and morose and so very alone. Aside from Dianne, they had never known him to have close friends.

"If you will see that he gets placed under the care of a competent psychiatrist I'll not object to a plea of *nolo contendere*."

"What's that?"

"It is a plea that neither admits nor denies guilt. The defendant throws himself on the mercy of the court."

Royce waited.

"If I don't oppose it, I'm reasonably sure the judge will fine Craig for drunken driving and put him on probation for a couple of years on the charge of auto theft."

"He wouldn't be put in the reformatory?"

"He wouldn't be put in the reformatory."

Royce sighed his relief.

Craig was jubilant when he heard the county attorney's offer.

"I knew you could do it, Dad."

Craig went out to the sale barn to see his boss as soon as he was released from jail. At first it seemed that he would lose his job; but when he assured Mr. Long that it would not happen again, he was given another chance.

"But I think you'd better wait to start work until after

131

you've seen the doctor in Omaha," the sale-barn owner said.

Craig squinted narrowly. "You know about that?"

"Everybody in Glenville knows about that."

The earliest Royce was able to get an appointment with the psychiatrist their local doctor recommended was Monday morning. He and Penny took Craig to Omaha Sunday afternoon.

"Does *she* have to go along?" he demanded, contempt twisting his mouth.

"Yes, Mother has to go along," Royce repeated, his own anger smoking darkly in his eyes. Craig knew that few things upset him more than a sneering reference to Penny as "she."

"For crying out loud! Just once I'd like to do something with you without having *her* tag along."

Royce did not answer him.

After a preliminary examination in the doctor's office, he asked that Craig be admitted to the hospital so he could perform more extensive tests.

"It might take a week or ten days to complete the examination. I'd like to give him a thorough physical, including a brain-wave test and a thorough psychiatric examination."

An examination like that ought to show the people in Glenville who were getting such enjoyment out of gossiping about Craig that there actually was something wrong with him. Maybe that would help them to understand him and his problems a little better. The psychiatrist was one of the best in the state; surely he would be able to get to the bottom of Craig's troubles.

Just knowing that his son was getting psychiatric help was enough to ease some of the pain that churned within Royce. If there was some psychological basis for his delinquency, Craig couldn't be blamed for it. He and Penny couldn't be blamed for it either, any more than parents could be blamed for a son's broken leg. It was one of those things that happened without anyone in particular being responsible. Believing that helped Royce through the next few days.

Early in the next week the psychiatrist called and asked Royce and Penny to come down. There was some deviation in the brain-wave test that indicated slight damage, but he found nothing else physically wrong with Craig.

"Is that good news or bad?" Penny asked.

"It's good news in that we don't have to concern ourselves with physical problems, but your son does have some decidedly antisocial behavior characteristics."

Royce shuddered.

"Do you think you can do anything for him?"

"Perhaps." The smile was evasive. "And, perhaps not. It's one of those things that is most difficult to predict with any degree of certainty. This may end your problems, or it may simply signal the beginning of them."

Craig didn't seem to care whether he went home with them or not. He slouched in the corner of the back seat, scowling. And, if he could avoid it, he didn't even answer them.

It was different when he got home and called Dianne. His smile cracked the petulant frown on his face and his eyes danced.

"What do you know? She's not mad at me anymore. She says I can come over and see her tomorrow night."

Royce was as relieved as Craig. He had been concerned about what might happen if she refused to go with him any more.

"You won't find a better girl anywhere."

"You can say that again!"

Although Craig brightened markedly after talking with Dianne, he was still arrogant to his parents. He saw that they were quiet and concerned and chided them for it.

"What's the matter?" he demanded at the supper table. "Can't you talk?"

"There's not a whole lot to talk about," his Dad replied.

"Oh, sure." Craig's lips curled bitterly. "You can talk about what a terrible, no-good character I am."

Hurt flamed in Penny's tender blue eyes.

133

"Don't even say that, Craig. You know we don't feel that way. We're concerned about you, that's true, but it's only because we love you."

His face twisted into an ugly caricature. "I'll bet!" he exploded. "I'll just bet! You probably wish I'd go so far away you'd never have to see or hear of me again!"

Royce and Penny said nothing to each other about Craig's bitter self-pity. They had long since said everything there was to say about it. But they were both disturbed, even when Sam and Helen Montgomery came over to visit later in the evening.

Sam Montgomery was a big, tender-hearted individual who had only been a Christian a couple of years. Helen had been raised by believing parents, rebelled against the strict, unbending discipline that was her heritage, and only since Sam became a Christian had she become concerned about living the way a believer should.

The Montgomerys knew of the trouble Royce and Penny had been having with Craig and, as soon as they learned the Lawsons were back, they came over to see them. It was not curiosity with them. They were genuinely concerned. Penny did not share Royce's assurance that everything was going to be all right now that Craig was getting psychiatric treatment, and she blurted out her continued uneasiness.

"I know I should trust him more than I do, but I can't help it. I just don't."

Sam unhinged his big frame and collapsed in a chair across from her.

"Why don't we talk with the Lord about it?"

The way he spoke irritated Royce briefly. "We have been! We pray for Craig every time we think about him!"

"I know that." Sam's big grin wiped away his friend's irritation. "We pray for him too. But the Bible tells us we ought to get together and pray for each other, doesn't it?"

Royce nodded.

Strange a new Christian would have to mention something like this to them. He and Penny had been on their knees countless times, beseeching God to intervene for their son, but this was the first time they had ever thought about praying with anyone else outside of prayer meeting. Gratefully he and Penny knelt in the living room with Sam and Helen Montgomery to talk to God about Craig.

When they finished, Royce felt as though a portion of the burden had been lifted. It had been years since he felt so close to God, so completely in His hands.

Sam clamped his big fingers on Royce's shoulder.

"I've been wanting to get together with someone to pray about some of the people in our family ever since I got things straightened out between God and me," he said. "This was great."

Penny felt the same way. Over a cup of coffee she suggested that they get together the following week after prayer meeting at one home or the other to pray for Craig and others among their families.

"Sounds great to me!" Sam broke in. "Helen and I have a list as long as your arm of people to pray for." He set his cup back on the table and hitched his chair closer.

So, while Craig went to Omaha every week to visit the psychiatrist, Royce and Penny met with the Montgomerys after prayer meeting every week for the express purpose of asking God to intervene in his life. All four of them were concerned about prayer meeting at church and attended regularly. But now that they were getting together for prayer afterward as well, it took on new meaning for them. They were there without fail.

The pastor soon learned that he would have at least one unspoken prayer request. As soon as he asked if there were unspoken requests, Royce's hand would go up. Everybody knew he was asking for prayer for Craig. Even the pastor was aware of it. But he did not mention his son by name and the others remained silent. As often as not when Royce prayed aloud, his voice broke unnaturally. There was an agony during those days that he had never known was possible for a person to endure, and only their weekly times of prayer made it possible for him to carry on.

There was little in Craig's actions to indicate whether the

doctor's treatment was beginning to have any effect one way or another. Royce, who was grasping at every wisp of change, noted gratefully that Craig seemed somewhat more subdued than before. And, except for the nights he was with Dianne, he was home almost every evening.

They weren't surprised when Craig came home to tell them proudly that he was engaged. Penny threw her arms about him and kissed him impulsively. He scowled at her, but made no effort to pull away.

"I'm so happy for you."

Penny wanted to know all about it. She asked him about the ring, how long they planned to be engaged before they got married and where the wedding would take place.

"How do I know? Dianne has to talk to her mother about it first. She's got some stupid idea about having a church wedding."

"I'm sure she would," Penny exclaimed.

"You surely want a church wedding, don't you?" Royce said.

"With all that fuss? Don't be stupid."

Craig insisted they be married by the justice of the peace, but Dianne insisted even more strongly that they be married by her minister. They compromised by being married by the minister in the chapel just off the sanctuary, with only their immediate families present.

At first Craig said they were only going to have Dianne's folks and Royce and Penny there, but Becky was so disturbed at being left out that Craig relented the day before the wedding and asked her to come too.

"Do—do you really want me?" she asked, her voice trembling.

A frown tugged petulantly at the corners of Craig's mouth.

"Listen, small fry, if I hadn't wanted you, I wouldn't have asked you. Now, do you want to come or don't you?"

"Do I want to come?" she echoed, eyes sparkling. "Of course I want to come. Who wouldn't want to go to her own brother's wedding?"

He reached out impulsively and rumpled her hair.

136

It disturbed Royce that Craig had not asked the twins to his wedding too.

"I've got a notion to take them along anyway."

"No," Penny said. "If he had wanted them to come, he would have asked them."

After a brief honeymoon, Craig and Dianne moved into a small apartment on the other side of town. For a time there was every indication that Craig was settling down. They seemed to be a normal and happy newly married couple. At Christmas Craig asked Royce to come over and photograph them beside their Christmas tree.

"Just look at that tree, Dad," Craig said impulsively. "Did you ever see anything so beautiful?"

"It's very nice."

He seemed disappointed that Royce didn't mouth the same superlatives he used in describing it.

"We never had a tree half as beautiful at home. I can tell you that much right now."

However, there were disturbing signs. At least they were disturbing to Royce and Penny. Dianne had to go to church alone, they were told. She went to one of the other churches on the other side of town, so they didn't know about that for sure. But they did know that Craig was spending more time uptown alone than any newly married young man ought to spend.

But Penny discovered the most disturbing development when she stopped to see Dianne one morning and found her making the beds.

"I didn't know you had company last night," she said without thinking.

Crimson flooded Dianne's cheeks.

"We didn't have company," she answered.

Penny paused, as embarrassed as her daughter-in-law. She had treaded into a place where she had no business treading.

"I'm sorry. I had no right to ask that question."

Dianne laughed nervously.

"That's all right. I have to admit that it looks queer." She pulled in a long breath and expelled the air slowly. "Craig and I had a little argument last night."

"I see."

"But we made up this morning."

"That's the important thing." Penny changed the subject, but the more she thought about it, the more disturbed she became.

She talked with Royce about it that night when he came home.

"I know Dianne tried to make it sound as though it was just a little tiff, but I have the feeling it's something more than that."

Royce was more alarmed than she expected him to be.

"Do you think we ought to try to talk to her?" he asked. "Or do you think I ought to try to talk with Craig?"

"Oh, no," she retorted quickly. "They're married. We don't want to interfere."

"But this sort of thing can lead to real trouble."

"They'll have to work these things out for themselves."

There was a long hesitation.

"Besides, it would be awfully embarrassing to go into a delicate matter like this the way it should be gone into."

Royce laughed. "I didn't expect you to be a prude."

Color crept up her neck and stained her cheeks.

"I'm not, but I'm not going to talk to my daughter-in-law about sex. Let her find out the way I had to."

"I just hate to think of their having trouble."

"So do I," Penny answered. "But a lot of young married couples have problems of personality conflicts and sex adjustment. They'll get them worked out after a while."

"I hope so," he murmured. "I certainly hope so."

14

CRAIG HAD BEEN GROWING increasingly restless in his job at the sale barn. He chafed at being held to regular hours and, especially after his marriage, he resented the fact that most of the money he made buying and selling cattle and hogs went to someone else. Early in the spring he quit without notice to become an independent livestock buyer.

"I've had it working for someone else," he boasted airily. "I'm tired of lining the other guy's pockets."

"Are you sure you've got the capital to operate with?" Royce asked him.

His grin was infectious.

"You let me worry about that, OK?"

Dianne was too much in love to question anything Craig wanted to do, but Penny was most concerned about the change.

"I can't imagine what Craig was thinking about," she complained to Royce. "He ought to realize that he has more than himself to take care of now. He's married and has Dianne to look after."

"He seems to know what he's doing," his dad replied mildly.

"You'd never quit a regular job and go on your own with no more experience than he has," she countered.

"Maybe not. But, then, I've never made much of a success of anything I've done either. I'm too conservative to take the sort of chances that have to be taken if a fellow's going to make a financial success."

"You haven't done so badly."

He stood and faced her.

"You don't have to defend me. I know my own limitations especially when it comes to making money. Craig's ambitious and eager to reach the top. You can't expect him to be like me. He's a race horse; I'm hooked to a plow."

"I'd feel a great deal better if he was more concerned about taking care of Dianne and seeing that his bills are paid."

"He's done all right financially so far."

"But he's never had a wife to take care of either."

Royce expressed a confidence he didn't entirely feel in Craig's ability to make more money than his wages by buying and selling livestock on his own. Yet it seemed that he was going to do very well. His lack of operating capital was something of a handicap but, in spite of that, he was shrewd enough to make money on practically every lot of hogs and cattle he handled.

"I've already made more this month than I would have if I'd stayed out at the barn," he would tell Royce, "and I've still got two more weeks to go. This is for me. I'll never work for anyone else again."

Royce was proud of Craig's ability to make money and bragged about it to his friends.

"There's finally one member of the Lawson family who knows how to make a few dollars," he would say, revealing Craig's latest profit figure. There had been so much talk about Craig, even among Christians, that Royce enjoyed letting them know that Craig was finally living a respectable life.

It was true that he wasn't going to church yet, and that bothered Royce. But his son was moving in the right direction. He would be settling down before long, like so many of his former classmates. Church would come later and, with it, a close walk with Christ. Royce made himself believe that was inevitable.

The only thing Royce didn't like about Craig's work was the fact that Dianne had to be left home alone much more than before. Craig went to sales within a one-hundred-and-fifty-mile radius of Glenville, and they often lasted so late he wasn't able to get home at night.

Penny found it even more disturbing than Royce did.

"I haven't said anything to Dianne about it," she said to her husband. "I don't want to get her to feel neglected. But it does bother me that Craig doesn't spend more time with her."

"I don't like it any better than you do, but I can understand it. Craig is so anxious to get ahead that he's working long hours now to get himself established. I'm sure things will be different as soon as he gets a little more working capital. With as little money as he has, he's got to keep it working in order to keep going."

Royce saw the account in the paper listing Craig as one of the new members of a local private club where members left their bottles of liquor so that they could be served drinks with their meals—something not possible in the public restaurants of the "dry" state of Nebraska. At first his temper surged. Someone had included Craig's name in that list to make him angry, he reasoned. They knew his stand on liquor and wanted to hit out at him for it. But as he read the account once more, anger changed to uneasiness. Craig just might do something like that. Although, he was sure that if Craig did, it would only be to needle him and Penny.

He called his son and asked him to come over to talk about it. Craig listened seriously.

"I'm over twenty-one so I don't have to answer to you or anybody else, Dad," he answered when Royce finished. "But to be frank with you, I don't like what goes on there any more than you do."

"Then why did you join?"

"There aren't any good cafés in town. If I hadn't joined the club, I wouldn't have a single eating place where I could take a customer and know that he'll get a good meal."

Royce knew he shouldn't say any more, but he couldn't help it. "Do you have to have the very best in eating places?" he asked.

Craig's carefully handled temper flashed out of control. "For cryin' out loud, Dad!" he demanded. "How narrow can you get? All the club is to me is a good place to go to eat. I can take a customer there and sit for an hour or two at one of the tables, talking, without being asked to move. That's the only reason I joined."

"Are you sure?"

It was all Craig could do to speak civilly.

"If I wanted to drink, I wouldn't have to join a club to do it. There are plenty of places to get liquor if that's what a guy wants to do."

Royce did not answer him. He didn't like the way the conversation was going. Craig was too quick with his answers—too glib and defensive.

"You don't have to worry that I'm going to start drinking again. I can tell you right now that I've learned my lesson as far as liquor is concerned. I'm through with it."

"I hope you are," Royce replied, choosing his words with care. "I sincerely hope you are."

During the next few months, everything went so smoothly for Craig and Dianne that Royce was sure his fears had no basis. He was apparently doing well financially, and they had a new car and seemed able to buy what they wanted. From time to time Craig indicated that he was ready for Dianne to stop working, and she was as starry-eyed and radiant as when they were first married.

Then Royce met an old friend of Penny's from Valley, Nebraska, in the hotel coffee shop. Although Valley was only an hour's drive away, it had been a long while since either he or Penny had seen Evelyn Bradley, and she had to be brought up to date on each member of the family.

"I suppose you knew that Craig is married," Royce said at last.

"Oh, yes. I saw him and his wife at the steak house in Valley the other night."

Royce's eyes widened. So far as he knew, Craig had been away from home since Monday morning. He couldn't have taken Dianne to Valley for dinner.

"You must be mistaken."

"Oh, but I'm not. I'd know that handsome son of yours anywhere. I remember remarking to Julius how handsome Craig is now and how cute his little blonde wife is."

Royce chilled. Dianne was both lovely and regal, but she certainly couldn't be called blonde and no one would have called her little except in jest.

"I wanted to go over and meet Craig's wife," Evelyn gushed, "but Julius talked me out of it. Said I would only be making a fool of myself if it wasn't him."

Then there was a chance that Evelyn Bradley had been wrong—a good chance. Royce was angry with himself for getting so upset over what he heard. It was only a form of gossip, although Evelyn Bradley hadn't been aware of it. She hadn't realized what she was telling Royce—there had to be some explanation. He couldn't decide that Craig was being untrue to Dianne on such flimsy evidence. At the very least he ought to give his son an opportunity to explain—to defend himself.

As soon as he could locate Craig, he asked him to come over.

He hesitated suspiciously. "What's the trouble?"

"I just want to talk to you."

"Can't it wait?"

"I want to talk to you. It won't take more than a few minutes."

Craig repeated the question.

"No," Royce snapped, his irritation showing through. "It can't wait!"

"OK." He sighed with resignation. "I'll be there as soon as I can."

Half an hour later Craig came to the house. He stepped uneasily just inside the door.

"What is it this time? What am I supposed to have done now?"

143

"I just want to talk with you about something that I heard today."

"That figures." There was a sneer grating in his voice. "You've usually got something to jump down my throat for. I'm getting so I hate to come over here because I get a two-bit sermon every time I do."

"You're not going to get a sermon tonight. I only want to ask you a couple of questions."

Craig dropped into a chair near the door.

"All right, shoot. I haven't got all day."

Royce told him about meeting Mrs. Bradley and what she had said. Before he finished, anger smoked in Craig's blue eyes and his cheeks flushed unnaturally.

"For cryin' out loud!" he exploded. "What kind of a guy do you think I am, anyway?"

"That's what I asked you to come over for; I wanted to find out."

Craig pushed the chair back against the wall as he got noisily to his feet. "Do you actually think I'd step out on Dianne?"

Their eyes met.

"Would you?"

"Of course I wouldn't! You ought to know that!" He was trying to get angry over it. His voice rose almost to a shout.

"Did Evelyn Bradley see you with another woman at the steak house in Valley the other night?"

Craig paced furiously across the room and back again.

"Yes, that snooping character saw me with a woman at the steak house in Valley." He spat out the words as though they burned his tongue. "But did she tell you who the woman was?"

"She didn't know. She thought you were there with Dianne."

"Well, for your information, and hers too, it was a wealthy widow who owns one of the biggest farming operations in this part of the state. And she's a huge buyer of cattle. I was trying to get a little chunk of her business. That's all."

Royce wanted to believe what his son told him. He longed to believe it. But, somehow, he couldn't. Not without further evidence.

15

PENNY, WHO HAD BEEN in the kitchen helping Becky with the dinner dishes when Royce talked with Craig, came back into the living room as he left. Fear gleamed in her eyes.

"I suppose you heard," Royce murmured.

Her head nodded in a quick, assenting motion.

"I heard."

Royce was kneading his hands nervously. "Did you believe him?"

She was silent for a time.

"I'd like to."

Silence wrapped itself about them, isolating them for the moment from the rest of the world. He grasped the arms of his chair with his hands and pushed himself to his feet.

"We can't let this go on. We've got to do something."

"But what?"

He hesitated uncertainly. When there was a problem his first reaction was to do something—to try on his own to work it out. Penny was calmer and less inclined to hurried and poorly considered action.

"What can we do, Royce?" she asked again.

"For a start we can get Craig and Dianne together and talk this thing out. We can get to the bottom of it."

But Penny did not agree.

"We don't want to interfere. That would only make things worse."

Royce paced before her, tension tightening the thin, straight line that was his mouth.

"I don't know how you figure that. If they're having trouble, we ought to know about it so we'll have a chance to help them."

"How?"

"By getting them to a marriage counselor, if nothing else." His consternation grew. "We can't stand by with our hands folded and let their home go down the drain."

Penny pulled him to the divan beside her.

"The kids know where we are," she said tenderly. "And they know we'll do anything in the world to help them. Let them come to us. They will if they need us."

Maybe they would realize they needed help and maybe not, Royce thought to himself. Craig, especially, felt that he was so self-sufficient he didn't need anything from anybody. It wasn't likely that he would recognize they needed help, or to seek it if he did.

Mechanically Royce went to the phone and dialed.

"I'm going to call Sam and Helen to see if we can go over and see them this evening."

They went to visit the Montgomerys and spent half the time on their knees, asking God to intercede on Craig's behalf.

Royce was still deeply concerned about Craig and the things he was doing. Actually, nothing had changed. Their son still gave evidence of living in deep sin. But their time of prayer with Sam and Helen gave him strength and courage he didn't know he had.

Somehow he was able to get through the next week, although he found sleeping difficult. When he closed his eyes he would see Craig sitting at a nightclub table that was loaded with liquor. Across from him sat a brittle, sophisti-

147

cated young woman, makeup hiding the harsh lines of her petulant mouth and masking the crow's-feet beneath her eyes.

He was not entirely surprised when Dianne called him at the office and wanted him to come out to see her.

He got his coat and stopped beside the receptionist's desk.

"I'm going out for a while. You can take any messages that come in for me, and I'll call them when I get back."

"There's a call coming in from Northrup and Stern this morning, and I'm sure they'll want to talk with you. Can you be reached by phone?"

He hesitated. He was about to tell her she could call him at Craig's, but that would only make her curious and start her tongue to wagging, whether she knew anything or not.

"I don't care to be interrupted. Just take a message."

The drive across town dragged endlessly. It seemed that he was only crawling along, although the speedometer showed he was breaking the speed limit.

Dianne was waiting for him in the living room, seated on one corner of the divan. Her hollowed cheeks were sallow and colorless and her sweating hands worked nervously. A wan smile lighted her face briefly as he entered the apartment.

"I'm so glad you came."

He crossed the floor with hurried steps.

"Is there something wrong?" There had been no need to ask that question. The answer was written in her drawn features and her tight smile.

"After I hung up I almost called you back and told you not to come."

His gaze met hers and held there as though gripped by some invisible force that could not be broken. At last he spoke.

"Is it Craig?"

She nodded miserably, and Royce saw that tears glinted beneath her long, dark lashes. She was struggling to retain her composure.

"I—I wanted to talk to you when you called the other night," she said, her voice quavering. "But at the time I didn't see how I could bother you with our troubles."

148

"You aren't bothering us." He pulled a chair closer and sat down. "You would never bother us, no matter how often you called or what the problem was. We want to help you."

She began bravely. "I don't know whether you're aware of it or not, but Craig's been drinking a great deal the past few months."

The words slammed into him—great, numbing blows that caused him to reel. This was what he had been dreading ever since he read the announcement in the paper that Craig had joined the private club.

"I'm not surprised."

"They had to bring him home again last night. He was in no condition to drive."

Royce passed a hand over his face in a nervous gesture. It was one thing to have an uneasy feeling that his son was doing things he didn't approve of. It was quite another to have it brought out in the open, to hear Dianne talk about it in words that could not be misunderstood.

She wiped a tear away but her voice was firm. It had been hard for Dianne to get started. Now that she was talking, however, the words that had been held back for so long, came tumbling out, one upon the other, as though there was relief in saying them. "I didn't want to get you and Mother involved; I knew there was nothing you could do about it." Her voice choked. "Besides, I thought—"

Royce nodded understandingly. Dianne was just like he and Penny had been on so many occasions. She thought Craig would eventually tire of his wild ways and come back to her. She was waiting in the desperate hope that he would come to his senses and become the kind of husband he ought to be.

"What is it you want me to do?" he asked uneasily, afraid she might be expecting him to work some sort of miracle in the life of his son.

She stared at him. "I—I don't know. I honestly don't know whether there's anything anybody can do." Her lips trembled and scalding tears slid from under her eyelids and coursed down her ashen cheeks. "But, Dad, I can't go on carrying this burden alone. I've got to have someone I can talk to!"

"Of course, my dear." He put his arm about her tenderly, in an awkward attempt to comfort her. Royce's own eyes blurred. He tried to assure her that Craig actually loved her and one of these days would come back to her in the anguish of conviction for the sin he allowed to come into his life.

Presently her tears stopped and she managed a wan smile.

"I can't talk to my folks," she said. "They wouldn't understand."

Royce knew well enough what she meant. If she had been his daughter he couldn't have thought clearly enough to understand either. Even though Craig was his son and he was used to overlooking his faults, he found it impossible to understand how he could be untrue to such a girl as Dianne.

"We've been praying for both you and Craig," he said quietly. "But we'll pray harder than ever for you from now on."

Dianne's head jerked up quickly and she stared at him as though she had never heard of people praying for each other before.

"Thank you," she said simply.

Royce wanted to suggest that they kneel and pray together before he left, but decided against it. She probably wasn't familiar with that sort of thing, and it would only embarrass her.

She followed him to the door, offering both hands to him impulsively.

"Thank you so much for coming over and listening to me. I feel better just for talking with you."

As soon as Royce got back to the office he started phoning for Craig, but was unable to locate him. It was night before he found his son at the club.

"So you want to talk to me!" Craig exploded. "Big deal! And I'm supposed to tuck my tail between my legs and run home just like Daddy says."

"I want to talk to you tonight." He tried to keep the anger from surfacing in his voice.

150

"Can't it wait until tomorrow?"

"No!" The word was clipped and compelling. "I've got to see you immediately. Tonight!"

"I'll come to your place."

"You'd better go home. I'm going there and wait for you."

Craig would have protested, but he was too late. Royce had already hung up.

Penny, who had been standing at her husband's elbow when he phoned, spoke softly.

"Would you like me to go with you?"

His gaze sought hers, drawing strength from her steadiness.

"I know Craig wouldn't want me there. He never wants me around anymore."

"But I want you. We're in this thing together."

She got her coat.

Craig was home when they arrived, sitting uneasily on the edge of the divan. Anger darkened his handsome young face and smoked in his narrowing eyes. He must have known what was coming and braced himself for it.

Dianne was standing in the far corner of the room staring at him, her face cold and expressionless as chiseled marble. There may have been emotion in it once, but now it was drained of feeling.

She spoke softly to Royce and Penny as they entered. Craig looked up at them, eyes thinly veined with blood.

"What's the trouble this time?" He was surly and belligerent.

"I think you know." Royce dropped wearily to a chair across from his son, praying silently for guidance. He had done a great deal of thinking about what he would say when he talked to Craig—the illustrations he would use to make him see where his drinking and carousing would lead, the Bible verses to drive home the importance of godly living. But now that they were facing each other and the time had come to talk, everything left him. He was numb and cold within; his mind refused to work.

"Is this going to be sermon 963 or lecture 321 on the evils of drinking?" Craig sneered.

"I'd make it both if I thought it would do any good."

"Exactly when are you going to get wise, Dad?" There was a superior, indulgent tone in his voice. "You've been preaching at me for twenty years and it hasn't accomplished anything."

Royce's lips parted but he stopped the flow of words before they began. Would Craig even hear what he was saying if he did go on? At the moment he was so discouraged he felt that it was useless even to try.

Dianne spoke up. "I think you'd just as well know it, Craig. I called your dad this morning and had him come up. I've told him everything."

Rage contorted Craig's even features and his cheeks crimsoned. He swore at her.

"Craig!" Royce broke in sternly. "That's enough of that!"

The boy started to retort hotly, but checked himself.

"There wasn't any cause to bring you in on this mess, Dad," he mumbled. "We're getting along all right."

"From what I understand that's not quite true." He gulped a quick breath. "Your drinking can only lead to a dead end."

"I wouldn't go so far as to say that."

"You may not be aware of it, Craig, but there's a great deal of alcoholism on both sides of your family."

"What's that got to do with me?"

"It might have a great deal to do with you. You run a much greater risk of becoming an alcoholic than the average person."

Craig jumped to his feet and stormed angrily across the room.

"That's really good!" he snorted. "My own dad calls me an alcoholic just because I take a sociable drink once in a while."

"I'm only telling you what can happen."

The boy's voice rose. "You don't have to worry about me. I can take a drink or leave it alone."

"Were you leaving it alone last night?" Royce hadn't intended to say that. It just popped out.

Craig shot a furious glance at Dianne. "Did you have to blab everything?"

"I said I told your dad the whole story. I should have done it months ago."

"It's true that you were so drunk last night someone had to drive you home, isn't it?"

Craig swallowed uneasily.

"And there's this woman you've been running with. What about her?"

Color drained from his cheeks, leaving them ashen. He tried to look at his dad but could not.

"What about this woman?" Royce repeated.

"She—she's just a friend."

"When I talked with you before you said she was a business acquaintance."

"Well, she isn't! She's a friend."

Penny started to cry softly.

Craig shot a quick glance at her.

"I didn't know you'd get so shook up just because I took a few drinks," he said lamely. "If it means so much to you as all that, I'll quit. I sure don't have to have it."

Royce leaned back in the chair but did not take his gaze off his oldest son. He knew well enough that Craig was just mouthing the words he knew they wanted to hear. He was in a difficult position and was saying things he thought would get him out of it. But Royce knew, as well, that it was useless to push the matter further. Craig's mind was closed.

Yet, he could not leave the matter there. He had to talk about Craig's infidelity. He had to try to say something that would bring him to his senses before his marriage was shattered.

"And what about this woman?" Royce persisted. "Are you going to keep on seeing her?"

"No, I won't keep on seeing her!" Craig's lips curled bitterly. "For cryin' out loud, Dad, how old am I going to have to be before you quit trying to run my life? Can't you leave me alone?"

He spun on his heels and fled to the kitchen. Royce followed him.

"This thing is more serious than you seem to think it is," he began, keeping his voice down so the women in the living room would not overhear him. "Dianne isn't going to put up with this for long. If you aren't careful, you'll break up your marriage."

Craig's gaze met his.

"Maybe that wouldn't be such a bad idea!" He stalked back into the living room and sat down, refusing to answer when they tried to talk to him.

Dianne followed Royce and Penny to the door when they left.

"Thank you so much for coming over."

"Call us any time."

"We'll be praying for both of you," Penny said softly.

They told Craig good-bye, but he did not reply. As soon as they were gone he stomped into the kitchen petulantly, and flung open the refrigerator.

"What are you doing, Craig?" Dianne called.

He cursed violently. "If you want to know, I'm getting myself a drink!"

He came back to the living room holding a glass in his hand.

"And just exactly what did you think you'd accomplish by getting Dad over here to chew me out?"

She did not answer him. She knew that mood of his; he only wanted to get a fight going.

"After a while you'll get wise to the fact that nobody's going to tell me what to do! Nobody!" He went to the telephone, draining the last of his drink defiantly, and dialed the operator. "Give me Sharon Keeler in Farnsworth—"

Lips quavering, Dianne went into the bedroom and slammed the door. This was the first time Craig had ever dared to call this Sharon Keeler from the house. She threw herself on the bed and began to sob.

154

Out in the car Royce glanced at Penny who was sitting quietly on the seat beside him. It was some time before he could speak.

"Do you think we accomplished anything?"

She did not answer him directly. "You certainly gave Craig something to think about."

Royce managed a flaccid smile. The very act of doing something, whether effective or not, was a release of tension. He felt better for it.

But when they went to bed he tossed sleeplessly, the whole ugly business churning in his mind. Raising Craig in the way he should go was such a little thing for him to do for Rita. He owed it to her to see that her son became a fine Christian man. For her sake he had to get Craig to quit drinking and running around, and to become the sort of husband Rita would have wanted her son to be.

But he hadn't been able to do it! He had failed miserably!

He swung his feet over the side of the bed and sat up. For a time he buried his head in his trembling hands. He had to do something to get his son straightened out! He couldn't let him go on the way he was!

Scarcely realizing what he was doing, Royce slipped to his knees in the darkness and began to pray.

* * *

The story of Craig's infidelity soon spread around Glenville. Royce and Penny only heard snatches of it at first, the muffled murmuring of people at their backs. Occasionally when they entered a room, conversation cut off suddenly and an embarrassed silence followed. Royce didn't have to hear what they were saying. He knew they were talking about Craig. He could read it in their eyes and in the guilty flush of their faces when they saw him. It was infuriating.

It was on a Friday night that the phone rang long after Royce and Penny had gone to bed. He got up and stumbled to answer it, fighting against the fear that surged over him.

"Hello, Dad." The voice was blurred and indistinct. "Guess who this is."

155

At first Royce didn't recognize him.

"Don't you know me?"

"Craig?"

"Who else do you think it would be?"

It was Craig! Pain stabbed into his heart. It was his son. Drunk!

"I've just got to talk to you," he slurred. "You don't know what it's like to live with that woman! You just don't know how mean she can be. She's on me all the time about something. I can't do anything to suit her!"

"Are you talking about Dianne?"

Craig swore. "Who else would I be talking about?"

There was a brief, aching silence. Penny had gotten up and come to the phone beside her distraught husband.

"Is it Craig?"

He nodded.

"Dad!" the voice on the phone continued. "I can't stand it any longer! I'm going to get a divorce!"

"If you keep on the way you're doing now, you'll get your divorce! Dianne will get it for you!"

"Nothing would suit me better!"

Royce was about to hang up when he heard a feminine voice in the background.

"Are you going to talk all night?"

Craig muffled the phone with his hand, but not enough to keep Royce from hearing.

"Shut up, will you? I'm talkin' to my dad!"

Slowly Royce returned the phone to its cradle. Craig and that woman were sharing a motel room! The blow was staggering!

156

16

ROYCE AND PENNY saw little of their oldest son during the next few weeks. He never came over, even when he was given a special invitation. His dad made a number of attempts to reach him by phone but was unsuccessful. He wouldn't come to the phone when he was at the club, and no matter how many times Dianne reminded him that Royce wanted to see him, he refused to phone or stop by.

They heard from Dianne that he was spending more time away from home than ever. They tried not to bring up the subject deliberately, but there were times when she seemed to want to talk about him. He usually packed a suitcase and left before noon Monday morning, and would not return until late Friday night. Then, as likely as not, he would leave the following afternoon, not to come back until Sunday night.

Royce tried in desperation to put Craig out of his mind, but that was impossible. He thought about his son constantly. People seldom mentioned him to them, but both Royce and Penny knew that everyone in town had heard the gossip about him, and most were repeating it.

Royce was at the office one Saturday morning, making a few changes on the house plans he had drawn for one of their neighbors, when a gangling, hard-faced stranger stalked in.

"Are you Craig Lawson's old man?" he demanded, eyes boring into Royce's.

"I'm Craig's father." The architect met his visitor's gaze evenly. "Is there something I can do for you?"

"You bet there's something you can do for me!" He whipped a check from his pocket and held it up. "You can make this good." The man's attitude was belligerent.

"What is it?" Royce asked, furrows ridging between his eyes.

"It's a check that kid of yours gave me."

Royce's eyes narrowed. This was the first time he had ever known of Craig giving a check without having money enough in the bank to cover it.

"If you want that kid of yours to stay out of trouble, you'll pick up this bum check he gave me."

"What was it for?"

The stranger glared at him. "It's none of your business what it's for. He gave it to me and I aim to get my money one way or another."

Royce took a short, quick breath. "I'm afraid you've come to the wrong place. You'll have to see Craig."

"See Craig nothin'! I've already talked to him all I'm goin' to. I'm giving you one last chance to take care of this. If you don't, I'll take it to the sheriff!"

"You can suit yourself about that."

The stranger glared ominously at him.

"You tell Craig that Garrett was here to see him!"

"If I see him, I will."

With that the stranger whirled and stalked away.

For a time Royce was motionless at his drawing board. His hands shook and sweat pearled his forehead. Craig had been in other kinds of trouble before—some of it with the authorities, but he had never before known him to give a bad check. That could be most serious.

It was some moments before Royce could regain control of himself. He didn't know why he hadn't asked the size of the check or tried to talk the man into waiting to see Craig before filing charges. It was as though something had stopped him from intervening.

Numbly he went back to his drawing, but the lines blurred before his eyes. The fact that Craig might be arrested on a bad-check charge stunned him.

At noon Royce phoned Craig's house and asked for him, but Dianne didn't know where he was or when he would be back. When she spoke her voice trembled so much Royce had difficulty in understanding her. It was obvious that she had been crying.

"Did a Mr. Garrett come to the house?" Royce asked.

"He was here this morning."

"I don't think you need to be so shaken up about him. He's much more interested in getting his money than he is in filing a complaint against Craig."

"I suppose you're right," she stammered, "but it seems as though it's one thing after another. I didn't know a person could change as much as Craig has. He isn't anything like the nice, clean boy I married."

Royce had to admit that was true. Craig had changed more than he was willing to admit.

Toward the end of the week Dianne came to his office. He put aside his pencil and pushed himself away from the drawing board.

"Hello, stranger." During the difficulty with Craig a bond seemed to have grown between them.

"I've got something I want to talk to you about," she said, glancing around uneasily.

"Sure thing." He stepped behind her and pushed the door shut. There was no use in letting the girl in the outer office hear.

"Craig's been pleading with me most of the morning. He wants me to do something I'm not sure I ought to do."

Royce flinched. All he could think of was the telephone call from Craig when he insisted that divorce was the only solution to their troubles.

"What is it?"

159

"He wants me to sign a note so he can mortgage our furniture."

"Why?"

"He owes this gambling debt," she blurted. "He gave the fellow a check to pay it and the check wasn't any good."

"So that's why this Mr. Garrett didn't want to go to the sheriff. You're foolish to sign that note, Dianne. He can't legally collect it, and he can't turn the check over to the sheriff for prosecution. You don't have anything to be so concerned about."

Fear gleamed in her eyes.

"Craig isn't worried about the authorities. He's afraid of what this Mr. Garrett might do to him if he doesn't get his money."

"What do you mean?"

"He said the gambler is a member of the syndicate, whatever that is."

Royce was unmoved. Such a possibility seemed so remote—so bizarre.

"That hardly seems likely. Those fellows don't waste time out in the sticks of Nebraska. They're in New York and Chicago and L. A. where the big money is."

"Craig says they come in for the horse-racing season. They've threatened to do all sorts of terrible things to him if he doesn't pay them the $250 he owes them." Tears glimmered on Dianne's eyelashes.

"I still don't think you ought to do it. Actually, I don't think anyone is going to do much to a person for a trifling $250. They would scarcely take the risk of being caught and thrown in jail for that."

"I couldn't bear it if they hurt him."

Royce was not surprised when Penny met him at the door and told him Dianne had phoned a few minutes before.

"She said to tell you she did not follow your advice. She signed the note so Craig could mortgage their furniture."

"I was afraid of that."

"And that's not all. She told me she went to the doctor this afternoon. They're going to have a baby!"

In spite of himself Royce gasped. This was something he and Penny had been looking forward to ever since Craig and Dianne were married. They both loved children, and the idea of a grandchild was exciting. If only things were the way they should have been! If only Craig was a sober, thoughtful, loving husband! But with the turmoil and unhappiness in their home, things were far from normal. Suddenly he was sick and weak inside. A baby now would only complicate the situation.

Penny, however, was hopeful that a baby would change Craig.

"You can never tell how a young man is going to take to being a father. He has the possibilities of making a wonderful daddy. This baby could be the thing that will make him see that he has some responsibilities and cause him to stay home and take care of his family the way he should."

At first Royce grasped at the same hope Penny clung to, but his own uncertainty began to crowd it out. He thought he knew his son well enough to be sure that it would take more than a baby to stop him from drinking and chasing around. Nevertheless, it was always a possibility and he prayed for Craig with renewed fervor.

Dianne, too, seemed to feel that the baby was going to be a catalyst that would bring her and Craig back together once more. The night she planned to tell him she was pregnant she went to get her hair done and squandered most of her check on a new dress.

Craig eyed her suspiciously. "Where do you think you're going?"

"I thought we could go out for dinner tonight—just the two of us."

He shook his head. "Sorry, I can't make it."

Tears came to her eyes. "This is a very important occasion."

"It's not our wedding anniversary."

"It's more important than that."

She put her arms about his neck. He turned his head to keep her from smelling the liquor on his breath.

161

"What is it?" he asked irritably.

"We're going to have a baby."

Craig's eyes widened. "What?"

"Isn't it wonderful?"

His cheeks flushed slowly. "I can't see anything so wonderful about it. Why did you have to go and do that, anyway?"

Dianne's lips trembled. "Don't you *want* a baby?"

He hesitated, and briefly that appealing, boyish look he used to have gleamed in his eyes.

"I don't know. To tell you the truth, I've never thought about it."

That wasn't entirely true, Dianne knew, because they had often talked about children when they were going together. Craig had always said he was going to spend more time with his son than his dad had with him. He was going to be a pal to him and take him everywhere he could.

And if he had a little girl he was going to see that she grew up to be a real lady. He wasn't going to let her be a tomboy like Becky. Little girls shouldn't be climbing trees and playing football; they ought to be playing with dolls and helping around the house.

Dianne hadn't argued with him when he daydreamed about his daughter-to-be. She knew from her own childhood that little girls were not as fragile as he believed or that they had to be so sheltered. There would be time enough for him to find that out when they had a family.

"I guess it wouldn't be so bad at that," he said self-consciously.

During the next few weeks Craig was more concerned about Dianne than he had been since they became engaged. He urged her to eat the right foods and scolded her for doing the heavy cleaning. Two or three times he called Penny and asked her to come over and help Dianne.

He still went to the club a night or two a week and, although she didn't ask him, she suspected that he was seeing the Keeler woman occasionally. But for the first time in months she began to have hopes that things would be different once the baby was born.

But as her body grew heavier Craig seemed to lose interest in her and the baby she was carrying. Gradually he began to spend more time at the club and more weekends with Sharon Keeler. When he did come home, which was only for short periods, his eyes were bloodshot and he smelled of liquor.

Dianne said nothing to his parents about it, but they saw that she seldom smiled. The wonder and excitement of bearing her first child were gone, and in their place was the gall of unhappiness and discouragement. Several times when Penny stopped to see her she was crying.

"You've got to get hold of yourself, my dear," she said firmly. "You've got your baby to think of."

Dianne looked up, eyes misty. "Apparently I'm the only one who's thinking about him."

"That's not true," Penny told her mildly. "You know Dad and I are most concerned, and so are your folks."

"You know what I mean."

Royce was the one who thought of taking Dianne to Omaha to talk to the director of the radio broadcast.

"Penny and I went to see Dr. Benson a few years ago, Dianne," he said. "And he helped us a great deal. I think he might be able to give you some help and encouragement too."

"I think I'd like that."

He called Dr. Benson the next morning as soon as he got to the office, and made an appointment for Dianne to see him.

"She's a Christian girl, but right now she's so discouraged and unhappy that she doesn't see any way out."

Royce thought about taking her to Omaha himself, but finally decided it would be best for Penny to do so. Ordinarily the hundred-and-fifty-mile drive would have been a pleasant one, but, not this time. Dianne sat stiffly on the passenger's side of the front seat, her long fingers clenched tightly on her lap. Penny tried to visit with her casually, as though this was a pleasure trip, but Dianne would only answer when she was asked a direct question. The rest of the time her gaze was fixed on the road ahead.

Dr. Benson greeted them genially in the outer office.

"I think it would be better to go into my private office where we can talk. Would you care to join us, Mrs. Lawson?"

Penny shook her head.

"I think it would be better if I stayed out here."

She half expected Dianne to insist that she go along, but she did not. Instead she seemed grateful for the opportunity to talk with the director of the radio broadcast alone.

"Hold all my phone calls," Dr. Benson told his secretary. "I don't want to be disturbed."

Penny sat down and picked up a magazine, trying to read. She could hear the muffled voices through the closed door, and once or twice it sounded as though Dianne was crying. Silently she prayed for their son's wife, that God would give her the strength and encouragement she so desperately needed.

Half an hour or so later Dr. Benson's voice came over the intercom to his secretary.

"Would you please ask Mrs. Lawson to come in?"

Penny laid aside her magazine and got quickly to her feet. As the door closed behind her she saw that Dianne was wiping at her eyes.

"Won't you sit down?" Dr. Benson asked. "Dianne has something she wants to tell you."

There was a new radiance about Dianne, a glow that seemed to transform her features.

"I just want to tell you that I'm a Christian now."

Penny gasped. "But I thought—"

"I know," Dianne broke in. "You and Dad thought I was a Christian. That was why I couldn't talk to you. I was too proud, I guess. I saw, though, that you had something I didn't have, and I wanted it desperately."

She went on to tell about her own pastor—how he would talk about walking with Jesus without explaining what he meant. On one occasion he said that being born in a garage didn't make one a car and being born in a chicken coop didn't make one a chicken. Being born in a Christian home, he went on, didn't make one a Christian either.

"I sat there clinging to every word," she explained, "wondering how a person could become a Christian. But he didn't explain any further. So when you and Dad mentioned my coming here to talk with Dr. Benson, I was anxious to come."

Before they left his office that morning the radio pastor prayed once more for Craig.

"We still have to claim God's promise that He will save him. It's there in His Word. We can *know* for sure that it is going to happen at some time. But we don't want to be impatient. In some lives God works slowly."

On the way home Penny and Dianne talked with even more warmth and closeness. It was almost as though they had just become acquainted with each other.

"Now," the girl said, "I believe I can go through having this baby alone, if that's the way it has to be."

"We'll pray that it doesn't."

Penny suggested that Dianne go home with her and spend the night, but she didn't want to.

"I think I'd like to be alone."

"You can call us if you want us."

Dianne laid a hand on her arm. "Thank you so much for everything."

Tears flooded Penny's eyes.

Before Dianne got out of the car Penny suggested that they meet for Bible study and prayer once a week. The girl agreed eagerly.

Penny soon found that Dianne's interest in the Bible was genuine. Their hourly sessions soon were two and three hours long, and from time to time during the week she would call Penny to ask about something she had been reading.

"You know, I didn't realize it until we started to study together, but I didn't learn anything about the Bible in all the years I've gone to Sunday school. We just don't use the Bible in our church the way you do."

Craig was gone for several days, but when he came home Dianne told him what she had done. She was prepared to hear his ridicule; but as she told him about her counseling session with Dr. Benson, wistful lights glittered in his eyes.

"I'm happy for you," he said with surprising frankness. "Sometimes I almost wish that—"

She waited eagerly, but he did not continue. Instead he leaned over and crushed his cigarette in the ashtray.

"I know you'll be much happier."

She hoped her decision for Christ would somehow make a difference in Craig, but it didn't. He continued to drink as much as ever and was still seeing Sharon Keeler or some other woman. She found evidences of it in his pockets when she sent his clothes to the cleaners—half-used lipsticks that didn't belong to her, and handkerchiefs with smudges of scarlet on them. On one occasion she came across a jade cigarette case that must have cost a couple of hundred dollars. Those things hurt more deeply than she would admit, but she clung to the hope that one day Craig would change. Deep in her heart she felt that would be when the baby was born and he realized the responsibilities of fatherhood.

Craig was away when the time came for Dianne to go to the hospital. When the pains were ten minutes apart she called Penny.

"I'll come right over. Do you have any idea where Craig is? Dad can try to get in touch with him."

"No." Tears lurked in her trembling voice. "There's only one place I would know to call besides the club and I—I wouldn't want to call him there."

Royce felt the same as Dianne. He couldn't call Craig at Sharon Keeler's to tell him the baby was on the way. He felt the old numbing ache in the region of his heart—a dull, spreading pain that lay heavily on his chest. What sort of man had he raised his son to be, when he would be out with another woman at the time his own baby was born?

Stephanie was born some twelve hours later. At first it seemed that everything was all right, but Dianne went into shock and almost died. Craig came home while she was still unconscious. He paced the hospital corridor nervously.

"Why didn't you call me, Dad?" he asked, his voice quivering. "Why didn't you get word to me that Dianne was in labor?"

Royce pivoted, sudden anger blazing in his eyes. "And just how was I supposed to get word to you?" he demanded. "Answer me that!"

Craig was silent.

"If you were any kind of a man at all, you would have been home with Dianne and nobody would have had to get hold of you!"

Craig's shoulders shook convulsively.

17

IT WAS SEVERAL DAYS and six blood transfusions later that Dianne was taken off the critical list and moved out of the intensive-care unit. Craig was at the hospital constantly during those long, difficult hours. He haunted the supervisor's office to get some word about Dianne and called her doctor at least twice a day. Whenever Royce or Penny went to the hospital he was there, standing in the hall or nervously pacing the floor of the waiting room.

"You know, this has been hard on all of us, Penny," Royce said, "but this serious illness of Dianne's might be the thing that will change Craig. He's seen that something could happen to her. Perhaps it's shown him that he loves her a great deal more than he thought he had in the last few months."

"This might be God's doing to bring him to his senses," Penny answered.

Indeed, as Dianne and Stephanie came home from the hospital it did seem that there was a change in Craig, a change more pronounced than any he had evidenced the last year or more. He hired a woman to come in and help her do the work for a time and was careful to see that she did not overdo.

"We're not going to have you in the hospital again if I can help it."

But, surprisingly, or so it seemed to his parents, he would have little to do with the baby. He looked at her when she was in her crib, but refused to hold her.

"I'm afraid I'll drop her or something."

The change in Craig continued for about two months. Then he began to visit the club once more, and it wasn't long until he was drinking and carousing the same as before. Only this time there was a significant difference. Dianne had been working up until a few weeks before the baby was born and, in spite of Craig's drinking, he had been able to keep the money coming in with surprising consistency. Now, however, their bills mounted. The first Dianne knew about it was when the people they owed started phoning the house.

She flushed with embarrassment even though she was speaking on the phone. She had never owed money before and was not used to the pressure they put on.

"You'll have to talk with Craig about it."

Sometimes they would try to pressure her to pay, but when they became convinced that she was telling them the truth and had nothing to do with Craig's business affairs, they concentrated on getting to talk with him.

"Would you tell him to come in and see me?"

"I'll tell him," she agreed. But, even as she did so, she knew it wouldn't do any good. Craig hadn't been assuming many of his responsibilities those days.

But when he came home she handed him the sheet on which she had written the names and phone numbers of those who called for him.

"You'll have to get in touch with them. I told them you'd see them as soon as you got back."

A sneer twisted his petulant young mouth.

"I don't have to do anything I don't want to do," he informed her archly. "I'm over twenty-one. I can do as I please."

She had to fight against the anger that surged within her.

"They said you've ignored the statements they've been

169

sending you for so long that something has to be done about them. They won't carry our accounts any longer."

He glanced at the sheet carelessly and stuffed it in his pocket.

"They don't have to get so shook up. I'll pay them as soon as I get the money."

Dianne knew she shouldn't press him, but she had to. The matter was too serious to let him shrug it away.

"All you've got to do is go in and talk with them. Tell them how our financial situation is and about when we can get them paid."

"I told you I'd take care of it, didn't I? Now get off my back, will you?"

That night he talked with Dianne about going back to work.

"It wouldn't hurt you to get a job, you know," he said suddenly.

She didn't know why it made her so angry, but her temper smoked in her eyes.

"I have Stephanie to take care of, remember? Or have you completely forgotten that we have a daughter?"

"It wasn't my idea."

"It wasn't mine either!"

"You can get a baby-sitter, can't you? There isn't any law against that."

"Maybe I could get a sitter, but I'm not going to. She's your child and you're going to support her whether you want to or not."

He swore at her. "If you get hungry enough you might be glad to go to work."

She fought against the tears that threatened to break her composure. She wanted to unleash all the frustration and anger and humiliation and hurt of the past two years, but before his taunting smirk she was silent.

"Just think about that before you go lipping off!" He turned deliberately and went to the kitchen to pour himself another drink. Later he left the house.

Dianne cried half the night, living over the things Craig

had said and reconstructing what she might have told him. At last, toward morning, she dropped off to sleep, but her rest was fitful and she awoke as soon as it was light. Craig, as usual, hadn't come home again that night. Not that she expected him; he never came home after they had an argument. She supposed he went to Sharon Keeler to pour out his troubles and exact a measure of sympathy. He used to do the same thing with her when they were dating and he had trouble with his folks.

The next few days Dianne thought a great deal about the wisdom of going back to work. It was true that a lot of married women were working. They had to, and Dianne didn't blame them for it. But, for herself, she didn't feel right about taking a job. When she and Penny met for Bible study and prayer the following week she asked for advice.

"What is your reason for not wanting to go back to work?" Penny asked gently.

Dianne hesitated. In spite of the fact that she was almost as close to Craig's parents as she was her own, she found it difficult to criticize Craig to them.

"He's been so careless with money since—since—"

"Since he's been drinking?" Penny added quietly.

"That's right. And he's getting so many bills that my money would be going to pay for things he ought to take care of. I'm afraid it would just encourage him to be more careless than ever about taking care of Stephanie and me."

"You're exactly right. One of Craig's chief problems is that he's never faced up to his responsibilities the way he should."

Dianne drew encouragement from the fact that Penny agreed with her. It helped her to stand firm as Craig tried to bully her into going back to work.

During the summer and fall his drinking continued to get worse. It was commonplace for a friend or one of the bartenders at the club to have to drive him home and help him into the house. At first Dianne struggled to undress him and half carry him to the bed. And when he was so stupefied

171

he couldn't control his kidneys, she would wrestle him out of bed to change the sheets.

After a while she simply moved into Stephanie's room when he came home drunk. She let him sleep in his clothes if he was too drunk to undress. The stench in the room from stale liquor and urine was overwhelming, but she was too exhausted, too defeated, even to attempt to clean it up until he had slept himself sober and was gone again.

She found herself looking forward to the times when he was gone and dreading the sound of their car in the drive when he returned. From those who frequented the sale barn she heard that he was not doing well financially.

"He must not have much money," one friend told her. "He isn't able to buy more than a few head of cattle at a time."

Her friend didn't say, but Dianne knew that Craig's excessive drinking was the reason for his lack of money. That made it all the more difficult for her.

Royce and Penny were aware that the situation was hard for Dianne with a drinking husband and a little girl less than a year old. Not that she complained. In fact, when they were around her, she seemed remarkably happy and self-assured.

But Penny wasn't deceived. She read signs that were oblivious to her husband. A glance in Dianne's refrigerator and the cupboard told her how desperate their daughter-in-law's situation was.

"I don't think there's milk for the baby," she said, after stopping to see Dianne and Stephanie.

"Surely things aren't that bad for them." There had been times when Royce and Penny had been short of money, but they had always had plenty to eat.

"I didn't see any milk and when I asked Dianne if she wanted to ride to the grocery store with me she said she didn't plan on going."

The lines between Royce's eyes deepened. It didn't seem possible that Craig would leave his wife and baby without money for food, regardless of how much he was drinking.

"We can't have them going hungry."

Before they took the groceries into the apartment, Penny slipped a ten-dollar bill into the sack.

After that they kept checking regularly, and when Dianne needed groceries they saw that she got them. It made a significant drain on their own budget, but there was nothing else they could do.

* * *

Part of Royce's responsibility as a member of the board of the radio broadcast that originated in Omaha was going out to speak in various churches, showing slides that told the story of the ministry. Requests came to the Omaha office and those in his area were sent to him. One week he received a letter asking him to take a speaking engagement in Hamilton, Nebraska, about a hundred miles from Glenville.

"I don't feel much like going," he told Penny, discouragement dulling his eyes. "Every time I go anywhere I feel that the whole audience knows about Craig and the wicked life he's leading."

"I'm sure that's only your imagination."

"No, it isn't. Practically every time I go anywhere someone asks me about Craig. And when that happens I feel like finding a hole and burying myself in it."

She grasped his coat lapels impulsively and tilted her mouth up to his.

"I know how you feel," she answered, "but we've got to carry on."

"I know." Weariness spilled into his voice. "But there are times when I wonder why."

He wanted Penny to go with him. Usually they did go together, but something came up at the last minute to keep her home. He was changing his clothes when the phone rang and Penny answered it. He had finished dressing when she came back into the bedroom.

"That was Dianne," she said simply.

Royce read the concern in his wife's eyes.

"What's wrong now?"

"She was listening to the news from the Hamilton radio

173

station. Craig is in jail there for being drunk and disorderly following a fight in one of the local taverns."

Royce's face blanched. "No!"

"It happened last night. The other fellow is out on bail, but they are still holding Craig."

He grasped the foot of the bed for support. His head began to ache and that dull, heavy pain came back to his chest.

"Did—did Dianne want me to do anything about it?"

She shook her head. "On the contrary. She asked that we leave him there."

"What!"

"She doesn't want us to get him out."

Weakly he sat on the side of the bed. He couldn't go against Dianne's wishes; she had suffered too much on Craig's account for him to take Craig's side against her.

It wasn't the first time his son had been in jail, but always before Royce rushed to his rescue. Maybe it was better Dianne's way. His mind was so confused at the moment he could scarcely think. For a long while he sat on the side of the bed, staring at the floor.

"Don't you think you should hurry?" Penny said at last. "You have a hundred miles to drive and you shouldn't be late."

He raised his head helplessly.

"Every person in that audience will know about Craig. How can I go there and speak?" His voice choked.

"I wish I could go with you."

"I'm going to call them and tell them I won't be able to come."

"You can't do that! They're depending on you."

They were still talking when the phone rang.

"It's Sam Montgomery," she called from the living room. "He heard the news too, and wants to know if you'd like to have him go along."

Royce accepted his offer gratefully.

They were almost halfway to Hamilton when Sam began to tell Royce something he had been thinking a great deal about the past few days.

"I don't know whether this is scriptural or not, but the other night Helen and I were reading the story of Abraham taking Isaac to the altar and laying him on it ready to sacrifice him. He actually would have done it if God hadn't stayed his hand because he trusted God so completely."

Royce had heard that story countless times.

"You know, Abraham placed Issac completely in God's hands," Sam went on. "He could do whatever He wanted to with him, as far as Abraham was concerned."

Royce didn't quite see the parallel, but he had often wondered how Abraham could have done what he did.

"You've got to do the same thing with Craig. You've got to place him on the altar just as Abraham put Isaac on the altar. You've got to tell God that you're going to take your hands off and let Him do whatever He wants to do with your son."

He thought about that as he drove. It was a completely new and different concept to him. The more he considered it, however, the more logical it was.

That night when he got back home Penny was waiting up for him.

"Did you see Craig?"

"I couldn't after Dianne asked me not to."

She put her arms around him and together they walked to the divan and sat down.

"You know, Sam told me something tonight that really makes sense."

She waited for him to continue.

"We've been putting our trust in people to help get Craig straightened out."

"I don't believe I follow you."

"We took him out of public school and put him in the military academy in Oklahoma; we were depending on them to accomplish something in his life. Later we sent him to the psychiatrist. We've been looking to men and their knowledge and wisdom to make Craig become what he ought to be. Actually, all the help we've sought from men hasn't been able to do very much for him."

Penny knew what he was talking about. She had been thinking much the same thing the past few weeks.

"Sam asked if I didn't think we ought to put Craig on the altar the way Abraham did with Isaac." He went on to explain what their friend had said. "I've never thought of that before, but the more I do think about it the more it makes sense."

She was thinking of her husband when she spoke. "It's not going to be easy."

He was silent for a time. It wasn't going to be easy to turn the burden of Craig over to God. It wasn't going to be easy to say, with Abraham, that he was ready to leave his son in God's hands, that he was ready to let God do whatever He wished with his son.

Slowly he sank to his knees and Penny knelt beside him. Emotion choked his voice as he prayed the prayer of the sincere seeker. "Lord, I believe. Help Thou mine unbelief."

When Royce finished, Penny prayed quietly, asking God to give them the courage and trust they needed to leave their son completely in His hands. Royce was quieter and more relaxed after they finished, but concern still churned within him and that night he tossed sleeplessly. He had not yet fallen asleep when the first faint gray streaks of morning lighted the eastern sky.

By this time Royce and Penny were buying most of Dianne and Stephanie's groceries and helping with some of the other more pressing bills. That, in itself, was bad enough, but the way he was treating her was even worse. He never took her anywhere and seldom even spoke to her, except to complain or curse her for something she hadn't done. And occasionally when Penny stopped by their apartment, she would see a large, livid bruise on Dianne's face or arm. Once there was a dark half-moon under one eye, mute evidence of Craig's ugly temper. Dianne never mentioned that Craig had struck her and neither did Penny, not even to Royce. There was nothing he could do about it, except to lie awake worrying.

At last, however, Dianne reached the place where she

could stand it no longer. She came to Royce and Penny and told them of her decision.

"I've decided to sue Craig for divorce!"

Royce expelled his breath slowly, his gaze seeking Dianne's. An icy desolation surged over him, leaving him numb and lifeless. Briefly his mind refused to function.

Divorce! It couldn't be! Not in their family! The agony of the last few years had scarred all of them. Divorce would solve nothing except to make the wounds deeper and harder to bear.

Yet, what could he say to the distraught girl before him? She had tried so hard to be a good wife and mother. She had tried so hard to make their marriage work, suffering the shame and humiliation Craig heaped upon her without complaint. How could he ask her to stay with his son the way things were? A desperate, unspoken prayer for help escaped the confines of his tortured heart.

Dianne shifted her gaze to Penny. "I wanted to tell you what I'm going to do so you won't find it out by reading it in the papers.

The silence became a gulf between them. Dianne's slender fingers entangled nervously.

"I can't go on the way things are." Her voice was so soft they had to lean forward to catch the words. "If I don't do something I'm afraid I'll go out of my mind."

Royce's head nodded almost imperceptibly in assent. Both Penny and Dianne were eyeing him, waiting for him to speak. He cleared his throat.

"I know a little of what you've gone through the last couple of years, and I know how I would feel if Becky was married to someone who treated her and the baby the way Craig treats you and Stephanie. Both Penny and I have seen that things can't go on the way they are. We've marveled that you've stayed with Craig as long as you have."

A wan smile lifted one corner of her mouth, and the muscles of her body seemed to relax slightly.

"I knew you'd understand."

He hesitated. He hadn't meant to give her the impression

177

that he approved of divorce and was giving his sanction to it. He intended only to indicate that he understood the problem.

"But do you think divorce would solve anything?" he asked.

She flinched as though he had slapped her across the mouth. Anger mingled with the hurt that smoldered in her sad eyes.

"I thought you understood. You said you realized we can't go on this way."

"We do," Penny broke in tenderly.

"What I'm trying to say," Royce continued, fumbling in his efforts to explain, "is that I don't think divorce is the answer. According to the way I understand the Scriptures, God established marriage to last for life."

Her mouth became a thin, straight line.

"What do you say about those verses that indicate adultery is the basis for divorce?" she demanded, her temper building. "Throw them out of the Bible?"

He did not answer her. He knew his own interpretation of the verses in question. He remembered talking about them with Dr. Benson who believed that Jesus was only restating Moses' original permissive law on divorce, and that believers are not living under law but under grace. He had a booklet by the radio pastor in his study that explained in detail, but he did not get it. Dianne was too distraught, too torn apart by the situation in which she found herself for them to expound theology to her.

"I'll go over my understanding of that portion of Scripture with you sometime, Dianne," he said as gently as possible. "But I don't want to argue about it. What I'm trying to say is that I don't think divorce is the answer. You could accomplish the same thing by separate maintenance."

Her attractive young face clouded.

"What's that?"

"You'd have to ask a lawyer to explain it to you, but, briefly, you can keep Craig from coming to the house and bothering you, and you can force him to support you and

Stephanie, but there would be no divorce. He wouldn't be able to marry again and neither would you."

"You see," Penny told her, "we're asking God to work a miracle in Craig's life and bring him to Christ and back to you and Stephanie."

Dianne's gaze hardened.

"I don't know whether I believe in miracles or not," she said stiffly. "And especially that one."

Royce tried to find words to comfort her, but how could he when his own heart was being torn apart? When the same doubts that Craig would ever change so numbed his own soul.

Dianne got up to leave.

"If it will make you and Mother feel better about it, I'll sue for separate maintenance."

18

WHEN DIANNE WAS GONE, Royce and Penny stood for a time locked in each other's arms.

"It doesn't seem real," he mumbled. "We were sitting here talking about breaking up their home as calmly as though she was discussing a new car or a piece of furniture."

Penny's arm tightened about the waist of her husband.

"We've both known this has been coming. Dianne couldn't go on the way she has been."

"I know." There was a faraway tone to his voice. "But that doesn't make it any easier."

The following evening Dianne stopped by to tell Royce and Penny what action she had taken.

"I'm suing Craig for divorce," she announced defensively. "I saw an attorney this afternoon."

Royce's eyebrows drew together. "I'm surprised at that."

"I can't help it." Her voice was flat and expressionless, drained of emotion. "You don't know what I've had to put up with the past few months."

His thin lips set in a bitter curve against the turmoil that surged and ebbed within. It was with difficulty that he was able to control his voice.

"I thought it was decided that you would sue for separate maintenance."

Her anger flashed. "That was your idea. I'm going to follow my attorney's advice. I've decided that I'm through with Craig! I never want to see him again!"

The pain came back in Royce's chest, a heavy, oppressive ache that made each breath an effort, each moment exquisite agony. He didn't blame Dianne. More than a year ago she had reason to leave Craig. He and Penny both marveled at her patience. But divorce! That was almost more than he could bear!

Dianne saw the hurt on his somber face and her anger softened slightly.

"I told the lawyer I wanted to sue for separate maintenance, but he talked me out of it. He said that it's a clumsy arrangement that doesn't solve anything. According to him, I'd just waste the cost of this action because it wouldn't be long until I would see the futility of going on that way and would sue for a divorce decree."

Royce knew her attorney; he was divorced and remarried himself. He would have expected such advice from him. He studied Dianne's taut features helplessly. He had never felt so useless, so incapable of action.

Dianne had braced herself for the ordeal of telling them about the divorce. Now that it was over, tears rushed to her eyes and she stifled a strangled sob. Penny gathered her into her arms.

"There now, my dear. You'll feel better if you cry a little."

Craig had been drinking when the sheriff finally located him to serve the papers, but the shock sobered him. He went straight to their apartment to talk to Dianne. She was standing in the kitchen doorway when he entered, her face an ashen mask and her eyes bright with anger.

"Hello, Dianne." The arrogance and bravado was missing from his voice.

No answer.

Halfway across the living room he stopped, eyes pleading desperately with her.

181

"Why did you do it?"

"Don't *you know?*"

"I've been a big fool, Dianne. I don't want to lose you and Stephanie."

"You're a little late to be talking that way."

"But—"

"You've had plenty of time to get us back if you really wanted us." In spite of her determination to remain calm, she was trembling. "It's all over now."

"Let's sit down and talk this out."

"There's nothing to talk about."

He reached for her hand, but she drew away.

"I don't blame you for being mad at me. I don't even blame you for wanting to get rid of me. I sure haven't been much of a husband. But you really don't want a divorce any more than I do."

Tears quavered luminously at the tips of her eyelashes.

"How do you know what I want?" Venom edged her voice. "I'd suggest that you go back to your girl friend."

"Her!" The word exploded from his lips. "I'm through with her, Dianne! I'll never see her again."

There had been a time when such a promise would have sent hope churning within Dianne. Now it was empty and meaningless.

"Then you'll have to find someone else."

"And I'll quit drinking! I promise, Dianne! I'll never touch another drop of liquor as long as I live!"

"Ha! That's a laugh!"

"I mean it!"

"If you have anything else to say, you can say it to my attorney."

Craig tried to apologize to her and get her to take him back. He pleaded for another chance to prove to her that he meant all the things he was saying, but she refused to listen. When that failed he went home and talked with Royce.

"Why didn't you stop her, Dad?" he demanded. "Why didn't you keep her from filing for divorce?"

"It isn't my responsibility."

Craig's gaze met his.

"You could have stopped her if you'd wanted to."

*   *   *

Christmas sneaked in on the back of a mild winter. There had been frost and the leaves turned and fell off, but only a light snow had covered the ground, and it melted before noon. Christmas decorations on the streets seemed strangely incongruous to Royce as he drove home from the office without a topcoat.

He and Penny had to pretend to be excited about the Christmas season because of Becky and the twins, but the specter of Craig's life was a cloud over a usually festive season.

"To tell you the truth, I don't much care whether we have a tree this year or not."

"We can't do that to the other kids," Penny told him. "We've got to be happy for their sakes."

Dianne was making little effort to observe Christmas that year. She bought a scrawny little tree and set it on the table in front of the window. But for her, as for Royce, Christmas was hollow and mocking.

It had been months since they had seen Craig, but at Becky's insistence Royce made a special effort to contact him and invite him over for Christmas Eve. Although Becky's confidence was unabated during the week that it took Royce to get in touch with her brother, Craig rejected the invitation.

"Nobody really wants me!" His lips wrapped themselves scornfully about the words.

"You know better than that. We all want you."

"Why should I be there?"

"It's your daughter's first Christmas," Royce reminded him.

Gall laced Craig's laugh. "She's going to remember a lot about it, isn't she? She isn't a year old yet. I suppose you want me to believe that she's going to be heartbroken if I'm not at your place on Christmas Eve."

Royce's temper flashed. "Well, you can suit yourself about coming home to be with us. But I can tell you now that

183

Becky and Dianne are going to feel terrible if you're not there. You'll ruin Christmas for them."

"Stop! You're breaking my heart!"

Before Royce left, Craig softened slightly.

"I've got a lot of things to do, Dad, so I don't know for sure if I can make it. But if it means that much I might be able to come over for a little while."

"There isn't anything more important on Christmas Eve than being with your family."

Craig's eyes slitted in warning. "Don't shove me! You ought to know by now that you can't *force* me to do anything. If I can make it, I'll be there. If I can't, I won't. So you can get off my back right now."

Royce thought he knew why Craig was hedging. If he started drinking on Christmas Eve he wouldn't come home. If he managed to stay sober he probably would show up.

Royce relayed Craig's answer to Becky without adding his own conclusions. It would be hard enough for her if her brother didn't come home without worrying over his being drunk.

"I just know he'll come," she said, determination firming her voice. "I've been praying and praying that he will."

She was still sure that Craig would come, even after they had eaten dinner and were waiting to open the gifts.

"I don't think there's any use in waiting any longer," Dianne said at last.

Becky sat near the fireplace, blinking back the tears.

"Couldn't we wait just a little longer?"

Angrily Royce dropped to a chair and stared into the Christmas tree. What right did one person have to ruin a time like Christmas for all the others? That seemed to be the story of Craig's life. He delighted in ruining the good times of his family; he did what he wanted to do regardless of anyone else. Royce knew they ought to be happy anyway, but how could they do that when their hearts were breaking?

He got the Bible and turned to the story of Christ's birth in Luke. Reading the account aloud was traditional in their family. Then they sang a carol and Penny led in prayer. After

184

that they opened their gifts. But there was a cloud over the little gathering—a cloud that was brought by Craig's absence.

Royce saw his son one afternoon between Christmas and New Year's, standing on the street corner in front of the liquor store. Craig saw him too. He could tell by the way his son jerked erect and turned, defiance in every move, to go into the package store. Wearily Royce negotiated the next corner and headed home. He had been almost gay a few moments before, but now the heaviness came back to his chest until he could scarcely breathe. Penny read the pain in his eyes.

"You saw Craig this afternoon, didn't you?"

"How did you know?"

"How do I know?" she echoed, frustration and bitterness spilling out. "I can read you, Royce. You ought to know that by this time. When I saw you getting out of the car I knew that you'd seen him."

* * *

For more years than either of them could remember, Royce and Penny had spent New Year's Eve at the church watch-night service. Traditionally it was a young peoples' meeting that started at 9 o'clock with a film or some good speaker, adjourned at 11 for refreshments, and reconvened at 11:45 for a brief time of prayer as the New Year came in. It always seemed a fitting way to begin the new year. Until now.

Royce hadn't wanted to go that night. He seldom wanted to go out anymore and avoided it if he could. But there were Becky and the twins to think about; he had to set an example for them. And there was Penny who enjoyed being with their friends even though he found it difficult. And so he had gone.

He didn't remember much about the film or what had taken place during the social hour. He talked with a few people aimlessly, making conversation. His mind was on Craig. He knew, all too well, what his son was doing, even then.

Craig would have started celebrating at a bar somewhere early in the afternoon. After half a dozen drinks he would have gone to a dinner spot for a steak and a few more drinks. By this time he would be laughing boisterously. Still later he would be in a night club with his current girl friend, both of them so drunk they would have to lean on each other for support. The night would end in a motel and another act of adultery.

That was all Royce could think about as they filed back into the sanctuary from the church parlors in the basement and knelt for prayer. He didn't know who prayed before he did, or what they prayed about. Indeed, he forgot that there was anyone else in the church except himself and God.

"Dear Lord," he began, his voice carrying throughout the sanctuary, "you know where Craig is tonight and what he's doing. You know how far away from You he is and the deep sin that's taken hold of his life. Dear God, just bring him up short tonight! Make him see that his drunkenness and terrible sin are leading him down the path of destruction. Make him see that he has to turn his back on the awful life he's living and let You cleanse him and make him whole—"

Royce was surprised as he realized that he was praying aloud for Craig. Always before he had been most careful to protect his son, trying to hide behind a carefully constructed façade of respectability. Whenever he was asked for prayer for Craig—which was often—he camouflaged it as an unspoken request. He was sure the others there knew the subject of his unspoken request, but they couldn't be positive. In that anonymity he took strength.

But this time it was different. There was such agony in his heart that he no longer cared who heard or what they might say. As he knelt there he poured out his heart to God.

A hush settled over the congregation when he finished. It was a minute or two before the pastor asked the benediction.

Penny did not say anything to him about the way he had prayed, but they were both thinking about it when they went home.

There was a change in the attitude of many church members toward Royce and Penny and Craig in the days that followed. A change that the Lawsons weren't even aware of at first, and had difficulty in assessing when they did note it. There seemed to be more genuine concern for Craig than they had seen among the church members since they began having trouble with him. Every now and then a gray-haired man or woman would stop Royce and Penny.

"I just want to tell you that we're praying for Craig every day," they would say.

It proved to be a real encouragement. Not that there was any valid reason for them to be optimistic. Craig was drinking worse than ever. The few times Royce saw him were most disturbing. His cheeks were flushed with alcohol and his eyes were bloodshot and swollen. There was a perpetual sneer on his face.

19

DIANNE GAVE UP HER APARTMENT the first of the month and moved into her parents' farm home a short distance from town. Twice before the divorce action came up, Craig drove out to see her. Both times her father met him in the yard and ordered him away. He tried to phone too, but when she heard his voice she hung up. After that she wouldn't even answer the phone until she knew who was calling.

Royce and Penny didn't talk much about the divorce, but it was constantly in mind.

"I can hardly face people on the street," he told her on one of the rare occasions when the subject came up. "Sometimes I want to sell everything we own and go far away where nobody has ever heard of Glenville, Nebraska."

She put her arm about his shoulder understandingly.

"We can't run away from trouble," she reminded him.

The pain in his chest was so constant that Pennny got concerned about it.

"I've made an appointment for you with the doctor," she said. "You're to go to his office at three this afternoon."

"There's nothing wrong with me."

"I'll feel better about it when I hear that from the doctor."

Their family physician read the electrocardiogram and scribbled on Royce's chart.

"You've got the symptoms of a heart condition, but there is nothing organically wrong."

"I'm psychosomatic, eh?"

"That's one way of putting it, but I'd rather say that you've been under a great deal of stress lately. Your body is reacting to it in this way. When you clear up your emotional problems you'll clear up this heart condition."

Craig called Royce from time to time to ask about Dianne and Stephanie. Now and then he came out to the house, determined that his dad try to talk her into taking him back.

"It's no use. It would only make things worse."

He stormed out of the house, slamming the door so savagely he cracked the glass. Sorrowfully his dad stood in the doorway and watched him screech away.

"If I could only help him, Penny," he said miserably. "If there was only something I could do!"

"He's got to help himself," she reminded him.

While Craig had apparently broken off with Sharon Keeler, there was nothing in the rest of his behavior that Royce knew about to make Dianne want to go back to him. He was still drinking as much as ever and rumor had it that he was gambling constantly. Royce supposed that he was working at least part of the time; he had to be to spend money for liquor the way he was doing. But he hadn't been making his support payments for Stephanie's care. He had always looked out for himself first and then, if there was anything left, he took care of his family obligations.

Dianne stopped at the office one morning just before noon.

"I don't like to have to keep coming to you with bad news, but I just came from the county attorney's office. I've signed a complaint against Craig for nonsupport."

"You know what that will do to him, don't you?"

"It will either force him to pay the sum the court allowed me for Stephanie's care or he's going to jail. It's as simple as that."

He didn't try to talk her out of it, and he wouldn't have

189

done so if he could have. She had a right to get support for Stephanie. It was not her dad's responsibility, nor even Craig's folks. Craig was Stephanie's father, so it was his responsibility.

It was several weeks before Craig was arrested. The sheriff accosted him in a roadside eating place some thirty or forty miles from Glenville and took him into custody. The authorities had the papers to pick up his car as well because it had been four months since he had been able to make a payment.

He called Royce from the jail and asked him to get him an attorney and provide bail.

"I'll see what I can do."

"And I don't want that old crowbait of a lawyer you've been using. Get me somebody who's sharp—somebody who can get me out of this mess."

Royce and Penny knew that Craig did not want them to go to the trial, but they went anyway, sitting far in the back where they hoped they would not be seen. They were surprised when the judge placed him on probation for two years; they had expected him to get a sentence in the men's reformatory.

"I want you to understand," the judge said, leaning forward to peer coldly down at the ashen young man before him, "I am not being lenient on you because I feel that you deserve it. I'm doing it for your wife and daughter. You can't make support payments if you're in the reformatory."

Craig shifted uneasily from one foot to the other.

"I want you to spare your family the humiliation of being a burden on someone else. That's the only reason I'm not sending you to Lincoln. Do you understand that?"

"Yes, sir."

"And if you don't make support payments regularly, I will ask for a warrant for your arrest, myself, as district judge."

Craig's cheeks flushed hotly as he left the courtroom. Contempt darkened his eyes as he stared at Dianne for an instant. Then he pivoted and stalked outside where his parents were waiting for him. He did not thank them for getting an attorney for him.

"You don't know how fortunate you are," his dad told him. "I honestly thought you would be on your way to Lincoln tonight."

Craig pounced on him. "Now don't you jump down my throat! I've had just about all I can take!"

Royce flushed but he got into the car without answering.

They drove half the distance home before Craig spoke again, a bitter curve to his mouth.

"Did you know Dianne was going to throw the book at me?"

Royce's grip tightened on the wheel.

"I knew she signed a complaint against you, if that's what you mean."

Craig drew himself erect. "And you let her do it?"

"I couldn't have stopped her."

"What kind of a man are you, anyway?" Craig's lips coiled belligerently about the words. "What kind of a man would let someone turn in his own son?"

Royce glanced quickly at Craig, disappointment and shame mingling in his gaze. He didn't know why he should have expected the trial to soften his son's arrogance and make him more pliable and willing to listen to reason, but he had. Now he saw that he was even worse.

"What kind of a man would let his own wife and daughter go hungry?" Royce replied.

Craig's cheeks crimsoned. "They didn't miss any meals."

"That wasn't your fault."

"Her dad's got plenty of money. He could take care of them and never miss what it cost."

"That's not the point. The law says that a man is responsible for his family. And if you don't support them you'll do a stretch in Lincoln."

"That would make you real happy, wouldn't it?" Sudden fury burned in his eyes. "You'd be rid of me, at least for a while." He turned to Penny who was sitting in the back seat. "And that's what you want, too, isn't it?"

"You know better than that."

He snorted his disgust. "Take me to the depot!"

"You know you're on probation, don't you? You can't leave the state."

"Suppose you let me decide what I can do and what I can't. I'm a big boy now! Remember?"

At the bus depot Craig opened the car door but did not get out immediately.

"Dad?"

Royce saw the expression in his eyes change.

"Yes?"

"Could you let me have fifty dollars? I'm flat broke."

Royce hesitated.

"You know this has cost us quite a lot of money."

"I suppose it hasn't cost *me* anything!"

The silence stood coldly between them.

Royce protested, but in the end he gave Craig the money. He shoved it carelessly into his pocket and got out of the car.

"I'll be seeing you."

He swaggered away.

* * *

Royce tried not to think about where Craig had gone or what he was doing. He was afraid his son had left the state, had used the fifty dollars to get as far from Nebraska as possible. That, of course, would mean one of two things. Either they would never see him again or he would come back, be arrested and sent to prison.

Royce also began to doubt that God would answer their prayers. They still met with Sam and his wife every Wednesday night after prayer meeting to pray for Craig, but it seemed almost mechanical. Their real hope had all but died.

It was some time before they heard from Craig once more. Even then they didn't hear directly. Friends of theirs from nearby Parker told of seeing him on the street.

"What was he doing?"

"He's out at the packing plant on the maintenance crew."

Peace swept over Royce in a great, warm, pulsating wave. God had kept Craig from breaking parole by leaving the state, and he was working. He had a menial job that surely would make making support payments a burden, but at least he was working. That was more than they had dared hope for.

Dianne seemed glad to know where Craig was and what he was doing.

"I figured he had a job because the clerk sends me the support payments every week, but I didn't know where he was or what he was doing."

Penny read the concern in Dianne's young face. "You still love him, don't you?"

Briefly she flinched as though to avoid a blow. Then anger sparked her eyes.

"Love him?" she exploded. "I *never* want to see him again!"

Several weeks after Craig began to make regular support payments Dianne got a job as a bookkeeper and moved back to town with Stephanie. Not long after that Craig called and talked with Royce. He wanted to know about his wife and daughter and asked about Becky.

"And, Dad," he said before hanging up, "I want you to know that I've joined the Alcoholics Anonymous."

Penny was thrilled with the news. "Things are happening," she said. "God is beginning to work."

Royce eased himself wearily into a chair.

"I wish I had confidence in what Craig tells me." That tortured look gleamed once more in his eyes. "But I find it hard to believe him."

"You shouldn't. We've been praying that God would deal with him."

His gaze came up to meet hers. "I didn't tell you. Craig sounded as though he was drunk."

* * *

There was a knock at the door one evening some two months later and Royce went to answer it. Craig was standing there, his suitcase in his hand.

"Craig! Come on in!"

He shifted his weight nervously from one foot to the other. "I—I just want to talk to you for a couple of minutes."

Penny came rushing up and threw her arms about him. He stood stiffly while she kissed him, but made no move to resist.

"It's so good to see you!" She turned to the twins who were watching from the far end of the living room. "Boys, do you see who's here?"

They nodded cryptically. "Yeah, we see him."

Royce and Penny and Craig talked for a few minutes about the things that had happened since he had seen them last. He was interested in the fact that Becky was in Omaha at Bible school and that the twins were out for football. He was vague about what he had been doing and how he had been getting along. At last he glanced at his watch.

"Dad," he said, "I'd like to talk to you."

"Fine. Go right ahead."

Craig eyed Penny significantly and some of the old hostility glittered in his eyes.

"Alone."

"Mother and I don't have any secrets from each other. You know that."

Craig didn't like to talk in front of Penny, but it was apparent that he felt there was no way to avoid it.

"I came back to tell you that I've had it, Dad. I'm tired of the kind of life I've been living. I'm going to quit drinking and do what I can to get my family back."

"That's great—if it's true."

Craig cleared his throat. "I'm going to start living the way a Christian should."

"Do you really mean that?"

"Would I have come back to Glenville if I didn't?" His irritation showed through. "I'm going back to my old job at the sale barn."

Over a cup of coffee in the kitchen they asked him to move back into his old room.

"You've got the other kids," he protested.

"Becky is away at school and the twins are in high school,"

Penny said. "You can stay with us for a while—until you get on your feet again."

Craig hesitated. "Dianne's going to get the idea that I've got to be under your wing. She'll think I can't take care of myself."

His dad disagreed. "Dianne's going to be watching the sort of life you live. Whether you're staying here or not isn't going to make any difference."

Penny called Dianne the next morning as soon as Craig had gone to work and told her what happened. Dianne tried to keep the excitement from her voice, but Penny detected it.

"I'll slip over on my lunch hour."

When she came she wanted to know everything Craig had said and if Penny thought he actually was a Christian.

"He seemed genuine."

But now that she thought about it the barest pinpoint of doubt pricked the far corners of her consciousness. Craig hadn't really spoken out with confidence in what God had done and was going to do for him. His confidence, as usual, had been in himself. He was the one who was going to quit drinking. He was going to live the way he should. There was no need for him to depend on anyone else. Not even God. He would run his own life, only this time on a straight and upright path.

Her doubt was so vague and indistinct she was scarcely sure it existed at all. Had it been firmer and of more substance, she would have voiced it to Dianne. As it was, she pushed it back into the outer limits of her mind, trying to ignore the fact that it ever existed.

Sunday morning Royce asked Craig to go to church with them, but he refused.

"Give me time, Dad. I've got to work into this gradually. I can't jump into it all at once."

"There's no better way of showing Dianne that you mean business with God than going to Sunday school and church."

The warning lights glinted in Craig's eyes. "You let me worry about that. OK?"

Early the following week Craig phoned Dianne and asked her to go out to dinner with him. He had been afraid she wouldn't, but she did and he was happier than Royce had seen him since the first exciting days of their engagement. Penny began to think that they might go back together after all.

"If only he would start going to church."

Royce did not answer her, but Craig's sporadic church attendance bothered him too. He looked back on the time when he first became interested in the things of God himself. He had such a hunger he would have gone to church every night had it been possible. He had longed for Christian friends and looked forward to the time he could spend each day with the Bible.

He knew that people were different and couldn't be hammered into each other's mold, but Craig's indifference disturbed him more than he let anyone know. Craig's inconsistency was still weighing heavily on him one evening as he and Penny went to the Sunday night service. A few minutes before he and Craig had argued hotly over the lack in Craig's Christian life.

"Sometimes I wonder if you really are a believer!" he exploded in exasperation.

"I don't have to answer to you, Dad!" Craig reminded him, matching temper for temper. "It doesn't make a bit of difference what you think."

Royce didn't know why he had gotten so angry talking to Craig. It wasn't that he wanted to have trouble with his son. Those explosions bothered him far more than they did Craig.

The pastor had been taking the group through a book-by-book study of the Bible on Sunday night, but that particular service he did something different.

"I want to bring a message on the keeping power of Christ," Rev. O'Conner began. "Turn with me to the sixth verse in the first chapter of Philippians. 'Being confident of this very thing, that he which hath begun a good work in you will perform it until the day of Jesus Christ.'"

The words leaped out at Royce. At the moment he could

not remember having ever heard that verse before, but it seared itself indelibly on the tablets of his heart. This was God's answer to him regarding Craig—His assurance that the time was coming when their oldest son would yield the last remnants of his will to Christ.

He didn't hear the rest of the pastor's message; he scarcely heard enough of the benediction to know that the service was over. His heart filled with thanksgiving and joy as he drove home.

"Look in my Bible at the pastor's text for tonight, Penny," he said when they were alone in the living room after the twins had gone to bed.

She did so.

" 'The verse I'm claiming as God's promise to us regarding Craig,' " she read aloud. "How wonderful!"

* * *

Then, without apparent reason, Dianne refused to go with Craig anymore.

"I'm sorry," she said coldly, "but I'm not going out with you again."

"Why not?"

"I don't think I owe you an explanation."

He froze at the telephone. It was half a minute before he could go on. "Is there someone else?"

"I don't have to answer that either."

"No, you don't!" He swore savagely and slammed the receiver in her ear.

Penny, who had been in the kitchen getting supper, looked up.

"Is there something wrong, Craig?"

"None of your business!"

He almost collided with Royce as he stormed out of the house. Craig wasn't home that night when they went to bed, but some time after midnight the phone rang and Royce answered it.

Penny knew it was Craig before he picked up the phone.

"It was Craig, wasn't it?" she said when he shuffled back to the bedroom.

He did not answer her.

"What did he want?"

"He wanted me to call Dianne and tell her that he loves her."

"At this hour?"

Royce's voice was flat and devoid of expression.

"He was drunk."

20

CRAIG CAME HOME in the middle of the following morning, unshaven and his face swollen and flushed with alcohol. He was contrite and defensive.

"I don't know what was the matter with me," he told Penny. "I didn't want to start drinking."

She made no comment. What was there to say when her heart was breaking?

"But it's not going to happen again."

"It seems that we've heard that before."

"This time it's the truth. I'm done with alcohol. It's never caused me anything but trouble."

As soon as Dianne got home from work he went over to see her. Reluctantly she let him into the apartment.

"You can only stay for a minute."

"All right, all right," he said impatiently. "I just want to talk to you."

Stephanie stood shyly at Dianne's side, her solemn gaze fixed on Craig. He held his hands out to her, but she shrank away.

"I see you sobered up."

"I'm sorry about last night." The hurt was deep in his

bloodshot eyes. "I shouldn't have called you in the middle of the night."

"I'm glad you did. It showed me I was right in telling you not to come around anymore."

He sat down on a chair near the door.

"I want to talk to you. Won't you sit down?"

Her voice was thin and pinched. "I'd rather stand."

"What happened?" he demanded. "Why did you quit going with me all of a sudden?"

"You lost the right to question me months ago."

"If it isn't someone else, what is it?" His eyes pleaded with her. "Why won't you see me anymore?"

"If you must know, I've been talking to Mrs. Ackerman who lives next door."

"You mean old lady Ackerman who's always testifying or whatever you call it in church?"

"She's a fine Christian woman."

"She is for a fact!" His voice gave the words an ugly sound.

"She said she was praying for me the other night when the Lord told her to come over and warn me about going back to you."

Craig's mouth sagged.

"You believe that?"

"She knows a great deal more about the Bible than either you or I do."

He shook his head incredulously. "Did you go to my dad or the preacher to check that out?"

"I don't have to," she retorted airily.

"If you're so sure it's true, why should you be afraid to check it out with someone who really knows the Bible?" he asked her. "If you want to, I'll go with you to any Bible scholar in the country and we'll see what he has to say."

Her lithe body stiffened and the worry lines, that had deepened measurably in her face the last few months, made her seem far older than she was.

"I'm going to have to ask you to go now," she said coldly. "I've wasted far too much time on you already."

He jumped angrily to his feet.

"All right! If that's the way you want it, all right! I can get along without you as easy as you can get along without me!"

"Then why don't you?"

Sorrowfully she watched him stomp out of the apartment and down the stairs. Tears filled her eyes and trickled slowly down her ashen cheeks. In spite of what Mrs. Ackerman said, that wasn't what she wanted.

She remained at the door, listening until she heard the engine start and the car roar away.

It was almost a week before Craig came dragging home, sober and properly penitent. His face showed the ravages of the long drinking bout and there was a livid bruise across one cheekbone where he had stumbled and fallen against the curb. He didn't say where he had been and his parents didn't ask. There was no need for questioning. They could learn more than they cared to know by looking into his swollen, bloodshot eyes. He talked with them about Dianne and her new, self-styled adviser and confidant.

"If you'd just go over and see her, Dad, maybe you could talk some sense into her."

"It wouldn't do any good."

He didn't add that he already had tried to talk with Dianne about the influence Mrs. Ackerman was having on her. Using Dr. Benson's booklet on divorce, he tried to show her that the intent of the Scriptures was clearly opposed to the private interpretation of Dianne's Christian neighbor.

"I think you'll find that Mrs. Ackerman was influenced by the fact that her own daughter sued her husband for divorce a few weeks ago," he said. "As far as I've been able to determine, that's the reason for her violent opinions on the subject."

Dianne's face had been white and the tendons had stood out on the backs of her tightly clenched hands. Anger had smoked in her usually mild eyes.

"You'd do or say anything to get me to take Craig back, wouldn't you?"

Royce hesitated.

"You can go back home and tell Craig his little scheme didn't work. He thinks he can con anyone into doing anything he wants them to do, and I'm tired of it. I'm through with him. I wouldn't take him back under any conditions."

He hadn't intended to make Dianne angry or to get angry himself. He wanted only to reason with her, to try to get her to see that she could be such a help to Craig if she would only be nice to him. He hadn't expected such an explosion from her.

"For your information, Craig knows nothing about this. I came over here on my own. I haven't been conned into anything."

Her features were still cold and expressionless. "If you've finished, you may go now."

He eyed her miserably. "I'm sorry, Dianne."

She gave no indication that she even heard him.

He left her apartment furious with himself. He didn't know why he couldn't be like other people and say what he wanted to say without getting all tangled up and getting misunderstood. Now things were even worse than before.

He didn't tell Craig about his talk with Dianne, however, or that she was no longer speaking to him. That would just give him something else to get upset about.

Craig called Dianne several times during the next two or three weeks that he was sober. Occasionally she would be nice to him. At other times she would hang up as soon as she heard his voice.

Royce and Penny didn't know how they survived the nightmare of the next few months. Their son gave every indication that he wanted to stop drinking, but periodically he would stumble and fall. At times they talked about asking him to move, but Royce knew he could never bring himself to do that.

"We can't allow this to go on," Penny said, making no attempt to hide her desperation. "He's ruining our lives and threatening to come between us."

Royce knew she was speaking the truth. He hadn't been

himself for so long he couldn't remember what it was like to smile or have a good time with the twins. He only saw them play football once all season, and then Penny practically forced him to go. The two of them didn't go out much anymore, except to Sam's to pray for Craig. And it had been months since they invited company in for an evening.

Penny was still welcome at Dianne's, but it had been two months since Royce saw her and Stephanie. He had met her on the street and spoke to her, but she acted as though she didn't know him.

Craig was blighting the lives of all of them and it wasn't right.

"I—I'll talk to him."

"If you don't," Penny replied firmly, "I'm going to."

Before Royce had an opportunity to talk to his son, Craig went on another drunk and wound up in the rescue mission in Omaha. The superintendent called.

"This is Pastor Jerry," he said, "Your son's here with us. He's going on our rehabilitation program."

Their spirits rose, but their elation only lasted two days. Craig was back home in that length of time, sober, but visibly shaken.

"I couldn't stand it," he explained to Penny. "The fellows were so much different than anyone I've ever been around before. I thought I'd go crazy before I got out of there."

"We were terribly disappointed that you didn't stay."

"You don't know what it's like!" he flared. "I wish you and Dad would have to go to a place like that just one time and have to spend a week. You'd find out that it isn't so easy."

He glared belligerently at her.

"All I get around here is static. I've had a bellyful!"

"Then you won't mind what I'm going to tell you. Dad and I have been doing a lot of talking about you."

"I'd bet on that!"

"If you get drunk once more we're going to have to ask you to leave. And this time we mean it. We can't allow you to disrupt our lives."

He stared at her. This was something he hadn't expected—a totally new development.

"Well, you're not going to have to worry about that. I'm through with liquor. I had a long talk with Pastor Jerry, and I'm going to live the way God wants me to live."

Penny did not know whether to believe him or not. She had heard promises like that before and they hadn't meant anything. However, Craig did seem more sincere this time than he ever had. He attended AA's regularly and, as far as she and Royce could determine, he hadn't been drinking. They tried to think that his days of drunkeness were over, but every time he missed a meal or was out late at night they wondered.

Then Royce had to go on a two-week business trip and decided to take Penny along. It had been more than two years since they had a vacation and he could see that she needed to get away. Besides, he didn't like to travel alone. They were going to Chicago first, then down to Memphis and finally to Fort Lauderdale. Penny had never been to Florida and looked forward to it eagerly.

Two days before they were to leave they stopped to see Dianne and Stephanie. The situation was taut and strained at first, although Dianne did answer Royce when he asked questions. By the time they left she was talking with him as genially as though there had been nothing between them.

"I'm so happy that things are all right between you and Dianne," Penny said on the way home. "It almost broke my heart when you two weren't speaking to each other."

"I don't think she wanted it that way, and I know I didn't. I tried to apologize for what I'd said—" He paused and breathed deeply. "I don't know why I have such a terrible time saying what I mean. I didn't blame her for blowing her stack. But the harder I tried to straighten things out, the worse I made it sound."

"I can understand her position," Penny replied. "She's gone through so much at Craig's hand, and especially his rejection of her and running with another woman, that she finally rebelled. I don't know of anything more humiliating or degrading to a woman than to have her husband commit adultery." There was a long silence. "I could forgive everything else he's done, but, frankly, I don't know what I'd do if you had an affair with someone else. I don't know whether I could forgive you and take you back or not."

"I know it's been tough for her," Royce answered, "and I don't want them to go back together on the same basis as before."

"I'm glad to hear you say that."

"But I do have the assurance that they're going back together sooner or later."

The worry lines deepened in Penny's face.

"I know you keep saying that, and I'd like to believe that it's true. But I'm afraid there's too much bitterness there for her ever to go back to him."

He drove into the garage and stopped.

"There wouldn't be so much bitterness if Mrs. Ackerman and the rest of the pious, well-meaning busybodies would stay out of it. But they keep advising her and she keeps on listening."

Penny was silent.

"Have you noticed? It isn't Dianne's folks who are so free with advice, even though they have a legitimate right to speak out. It's the outsiders who couldn't care less about Stephanie and whether or not she grows up without a father."

They went into the house together.

"I feel the same as you," Penny said, "but I do hope you don't say anything more to her. It will only cause trouble."

"Don't worry, I've learned my lesson. From now on I'm going to keep my big mouth shut."

"Now that," Penny added, "is the wisest decision you've made in a long while."

He grinned self-consciously. He knew his own shortcomings as well as she did.

Craig came in shortly after ten that night and was getting ready for bed when the phone rang and he went to answer it.

"It's Bill Mosier," he explained to Royce. "He wants me to come over. I guess he's got problems."

Bill Mosier was a fellow AA member who hadn't been in the organization very long and was still having trouble with alcohol. He called for Craig every now and then, and when Craig needed help to stay away from the bottle he called for Bill.

"Have you any idea what time you'll be back?"

Craig pivoted to face him, a sneer twisting his features.

"Dad, you should know enough about these things by this time not to ask a stupid question like that. I might be gone half an hour, and I might be gone all night. Bill doesn't even know how long he's going to need me."

He got his jacket and hurried out.

Royce came back to the bedroom where Penny was undressing.

"I know this is the way the AA works," he said uneasily, "but it always bothers me when Craig goes off to help one of those fellows."

Penny did not reply. More than once Craig had gone to help a fellow alcoholic and had wound up by getting drunk right along with him. That, she knew, was the basis for her husband's concern.

Craig didn't come home at all that night. He still hadn't appeared by the time Royce went to the office. When noon came and went without him, both Penny and Royce knew that it had happened again.

"What do you think about going tomorrow?"

"You mean because of Craig?" Penny countered, bristling.

"I hate to leave without knowing where he is or what he's doing."

"We know what he's doing," she retorted irritably, "and it doesn't make much difference where he is so long as he's drinking."

Royce winced. "Don't you *care*?"

"Of course I care." She grasped his lapels with trembling fingers. "But the rest of us are entitled to live too. For as long as any of us can remember we've fashioned our lives around Craig. We've gone without so he could go to military school. We've taken money we needed for other things to pay for his psychiatrist and to feed his family when he couldn't take care of them. We can't build our entire lives around Craig. We're entitled to have some peace and enjoyment, regardless of the mess he's made of his life."

Royce took her in his arms. "We'll go tomorrow just as we planned."

He half expected Craig to come home that night, but he didn't. There was no word from him at the time they left.

For a brief interlude Craig and his problems were forgotten as they finished their business in Chicago and Memphis. When they got to Florida Royce called home and Craig answered.

"When did you get back?" Royce asked.

"Lay off, will you? I don't feel like arguing."

"Is there something wrong?"

"I've got a little cold, but I think I'll be all right in a day or two."

"Mother and I are going to have to have a talk with you when we get back. You know what she told you."

"Yes, I know what she told me. I can move out this evening, if you want me to."

"That won't be necessary, at least until we get back."

"Well, thanks. Thanks a lot."

"What are we going to do about Craig staying with us?" Penny asked when Royce finished the telephone conversation.

"What do you mean?"

"Are we going to let him stay, or aren't we?" The warning signals were in her voice.

"You told him he couldn't, didn't you?"

"I told him he would have to move if he got drunk again." Royce was a long while in answering.

"You know that will probably mean he'll lose his job at the sale barn and probably default on his support payments again."

"I know our homelife has been miserable since he came back."

"I've never crossed what you've told the kids before, Penny," Royce told her, "and I'm not going to start now."

Her eyes pleaded with him. "Don't you think it's best, Royce?"

It probably was best, he had to admit, but on his own he lacked the courage to take such action.

"I know you're right, Penny, but you know how I am where Craig is concerned. For some reason I don't think straight when it comes to dealing with him."

"It's decided, then?"

"It's decided."

When they returned to Glenville Craig was still sick. His cold seemed to have gone down on his lungs, and his cough was dry and rasping. Penny was alarmed at his labored breathing and asked if he'd seen a doctor.

"No, I haven't seen a doctor," he snapped. "And what's more, I'm not going to."

"You need something for that cold. It sounds like pneumonia to me."

"I'll be all right in a couple of days. It's just the flu."

Royce was so busy after being away for two weeks that he didn't think about Craig until he got home that night and found him hunched in a chair, his breath coming in long, tortured gasps.

"That cold doesn't sound very good, Craig."

"I'll be all right. I just can't get my breath."

Royce felt his forehead. "You've got a fever too. You should have seen the doctor today."

Craig's hostility glinted in his blue eyes. "I can't afford it."

"You can't go on like this. You'd better get to the doctor whether you can afford it or not."

"I'll go tomorrow if I don't feel better."

The next day the congestion in Craig's lungs was even worse. He did not protest when his dad suggested that he see the doctor. An hour later he was being put to bed in the hospital.

"I don't want to frighten you," Dr. Morgan said after examining him, "but your son is a mighty sick man."

The preliminary diagnosis was pneumonia so severe that it had affected his heart, but the first tests failed to verify it.

"We'll have to wait for the results of the tests we're doing," the doctor continued, "to get at the source of the trouble."

In the hospital Craig was moody and irritable.

"Does Dianne know I'm here?"

"I told her this morning," Penny said.

"Will she come up to see me?"

She couldn't answer that question. Dianne hadn't indicated whether she would visit him or not.

"Why don't you talk to her, Dad? You can get her up here if you want to."

"I'm afraid you overestimate my persuasive ability." Dianne had just started speaking to him again. He wasn't going to risk making her angry.

"Are you going to talk to her or aren't you?"

"About coming up to see you?" Royce asked.

His son's lips curled. "What else have we been talking about?"

"No, I'm not going to talk to her about coming up to see you. It wouldn't do any good."

"Then you'd just as well go on back to work. If you're not going to do anything I want you to do, you don't have to come up here. I can get along without you."

Royce ignored his remark. "I'll see you tomorrow."

"Don't bother."

After a week in the hospital Craig seemed to be better. His lungs began to clear and he could sleep at night without a sedative. He began to talk about getting out.

"I hope you're out of here in time for the special meetings at church," Royce told him. "They're starting week after next."

Craig scowled but did not reply.

21

THE ENTIRE CONGREGATION was excited about the appearance of Dr. Harold Roswell at their church for special meetings. In evangelical circles he was an evangelist of national stature, and he had agreed to speak in Glenville chiefly because he and their local pastor, Rev. O'Conner, had gone to school together.

As the dates for the meetings approached, Royce and Penny prayed with increasing urgency that Craig would be released from the hospital and would get to the meetings. However, this was not to be. On Monday the doctor allowed him to get out of bed for a few minutes, but he wasn't released from the hospital until Saturday. He still complained of pain in his chest, a headache and a persistent cough. It was obvious even to Royce that he wouldn't be able to attend the final meetings.

Sunday morning Dr. Roswell did something Royce and Penny had never seen done before. At the conclusion of the message on prayer, he challenged the congregation to pray with him for specific individuals.

"If you are burdened for a friend or relative," he said, "I'm going to ask you to jot the name down and bring it up to me. I'll covenant to pray with you for that person this afternoon."

Royce was the first to reach him with Craig's name scrawled hurriedly on the back of an old envelope. Without any particular reason, he included their phone number below his son's name.

The Lawson family had been invited out that afternoon and were away from home for several hours. When they came back Craig was sitting pensively in the living room. The television set was dark and he had not been reading.

"Dad," he said as soon as Royce entered. "Do you know what happened this afternoon? That Dr. Roswell called me and asked me to come to the meeting tonight."

Royce tried to mask his delight. "Are you going?"

"Are you kidding? I just got out of the hospital yesterday and, for your information, I feel lousy." The arrogance in his eyes died. "But imagine an important guy like that phoning *me* out of all the people in town. You didn't ask him to, did you?" he asked suspiciously.

"No, I didn't ask him to."

Craig pressed the palms of his hands together in a nervous gesture.

"He sure must be a great guy. He talked to me for half an hour."

The icy pains in the pit of Royce's stomach continued to grow. This was one of the few times he had ever heard his son express real interest in an evangelist, and now Dr. Rosewell was leaving before Craig would be well enough to go to his meetings.

Before the evening service Craig came into the living room where Royce was reading.

"Would you call that guy and ask him a couple of questions for me, Dad?"

He looked up. "What guy?"

"That preacher."

"If you want to talk to him you'll have have to call him yourself."

"Call him up."

211

"I don't want to talk to him."

Craig muttered something under his breath and stalked away.

Royce and Penny took the twins to the final service that night. Afterward the evangelist sought them out and told them of the conversation with Craig.

"He called me again after dinner this evening and we talked for another half hour. I know God is going to answer your prayers for your son. Write and tell me when it happens."

When Royce went into the living room the next morning Craig was reading a New Testament. He looked up, spoke to his dad, and read several verses to the end of the chapter. Royce was about to comment but something stopped him. He talked to his son for a few minutes, but Craig didn't seem to be any different than usual, except a little quieter and more thoughtful.

Royce expected him to continue to improve, but his condition worsened and by Wednesday he was back in the hospital. By Sunday his heart showed marked deterioration.

"Actually," Dr. Morgan said when Royce stopped him in the hall, "he's in a state of heart failure at the moment. I wouldn't term him critical yet, but he is seriously ill."

It was all Royce could do to go into Craig's room and talk calmly to him after that. For the first time since his son had been ill he was genuinely concerned.

"Where's Mother?"

Royce squinted at him narrowly. It had been years since Craig called Penny "Mother."

"She had to teach Sunday school. She'll be up to see you this afternoon."

Craig seemed disappointed. "You aren't going anywhere else this afternoon, are you?"

Royce had been thinking they ought to drive over and see Aunt Sally. She didn't even know that Craig was ill.

"Why?"

"I'd just like to have you stay with me. That's all."

"We'll stay if you want us to."

Craig settled back on the bed, a smile lighting his drawn face. "A fellow gets awfully lonesome up here by himself."

Royce didn't tell Penny that Craig had asked for her. He half expected it to be part of some sort of a pressure play, that there was something Craig wanted Penny to do for him. But, if there was, he didn't mention it when they came to his room after dinner.

"Come over here, Mother," Craig said, holding out his hand.

She moved up beside him, taking his big fingers in her small hands.

"I'm sure glad you came to see me this afternoon."

She sat down beside the bed.

"There's something I want to tell you and Dad."

They waited for him to go on.

"I want to tell you both how sorry I am for the way I've treated you." There were tears in his eyes. They had seen tears in his eyes on a number of occasions the past few months, but not from remorse. "And I'm sorry for the rough times I've given you. Will you forgive me?"

It was all either of them could do to answer him. Penny bent over him impulsively and kissed him. Their tears mingled on his cheeks.

"When I get out of here I'm going to make it up to you," he said brokenly.

Silently Royce thanked God. The Bible verse the pastor used a few Sunday nights ago rushed back to him. "Being confident of this very thing, that he which hath begun a good work in you will perform it until the day of Jesus Christ."

Perhaps that was what was happening, but he couldn't be sure. He had expected some climactic scene, some great turmoil and resolve before Craig would become what they had been praying he would be. This had come about so quietly, so easily, he could not help doubting.

Royce sat there more than half expecting Craig to try to use this request for forgiveness to his own advantage, to ask them to contact Dianne for him, or one of his creditors. But nothing like that happened.

They sat in his hospital room for the balance of the afternoon. Craig seemed hungry to talk to them, to learn what they had been doing, how Becky was getting along, and the sort of friends she had.

"You know, Dad," he said, "you've got to keep a close watch on a girl's friends. She could get into all kinds of trouble if she starts running with the wrong crowd, and we don't want that to happen."

In one of the few brief silences Craig reached out and took Penny's hand once more. She was crying her joy as she and Royce walked down the corridor when visiting hours were over.

"We prayed for this change, Royce, but I don't know for sure if I ever really believed it would come about."

"We don't want to get our hopes too high. We've been deceived before."

She nodded, eyes glistening with happiness.

"We'll wait and see. But down deep in my heart, *I know!*"

On Wednesday night at prayer meeting the pastor surprised everyone by talking to the devout little group about Craig.

"I was up to the hospital to see him this afternoon," he began. "I'm very concerned about his physical condition, but I'm no longer concerned about his spiritual condition. He has the humble, contrite spirit of a consecrated believer."

In spite of himself, Royce gasped. Humility had never been one of Craig's attributes. Even as his father he had to admit that his son was arrogant, proud, antagonistic and overbearing.

The next morning Dr. Morgan called Royce and Penny into his office for a consultation.

"I wish I could tell you that he's getting better," he said, "but actually, he has made no progress since the day he came in here the second time. He can't continue very long like this."

Penny's cheeks paled. Royce was trying to frame a question in his mind when the doctor continued. "I don't know

214

whether you're aware of it or not, but we're dealing with a changed man upstairs."

Dianne had called several times to learn how Craig was, but she didn't go and see him until that Thursday night. He was alone in the room when she came in.

"Hello." Her voice was strained.

"Hello, Dianne." He spoke so softly she could scarcely hear him. "I've been hoping you would come."

She sat down near the bed.

"How do you feel?"

He did not answer her question, but raised himself on one elbow.

"I've been lying here the last few days thinking about how terribly I've treated you and Stephanie. Will you forgive me?"

Her body stiffened. It was coming now—the request to go back to him. She steeled herself against it.

"I'd give anything in the world if I could undo what I did to the two of you."

She saw the tears in his eyes.

"You really mean that, don't you?" she said incredulously.

"More than I could ever say."

An hour and a half later Dianne appeared at Royce and Penny's, her cheeks stained with tears.

"I've just come from the hospital," she said, the awe of encounter with Craig hushing her voice.

"Is he worse?"

"He asked me to forgive him," Dianne choked, "and I asked him to forgive me. I've been wrong in a lot of things too, you know."

They stared at her. It wasn't true. It couldn't be!

They knelt that night, tears of joy on their cheeks as they praised God for His faithfulness. To be sure, that didn't mean they were going back together, but it was a start.

The next day Craig had company in his room when Royce stopped at the hospital. One of his old drinking buddies was there. They were talking loudly enough for their voices to be heard down the hall.

"When you get out of here, fella," his visitor was saying,

"I'll buy a bottle of the best whisky in town and we'll really hang one on."

"Not me," Craig said firmly. "With God's help I've put all of that behind me."

Royce stopped outside the door. He didn't mean to eavesdrop. This just didn't seem to be the proper time for him to go in.

"Aw now, come off it!" Larry exclaimed in disbelief. "You've got to be kidding."

"I'm giving it to you straight. I'm a Christian now, and I'm through with the stupid kind of life I was living." He paused. "And if you want to know something, Larry, you ought to think about doing the same thing."

Craig was stumbling over the words, but there was no mistaking his intent. Royce knew he was trying to tell his friend what Christ had done in his life. Royce turned and tiptoed down the hall.

When he came back later in the afternoon, Craig asked him to call still another friend and have him stop and see him.

"I've got to talk to him, Dad. He's fooling around with God the same way I was. He's trying to get everything God has to offer, but is drinking and living for the devil too. I want to warn him that a life like that is no good—that God won't let him keep on like that forever."

Royce did not go to the hospital to see his son that night. He stayed in his study and wrote to Dr. Roswell. He didn't draw any conclusions about the change that had come over Craig; he simply related what was taking place.

Dear Dr. Roswell:

You asked me to drop you a line when there had been a spiritual change in our son Craig. Apparently that time has come. I say apparently, not because I lack the faith to believe God could bring this about, but because it requires a certain amount of judgment on my part to make the statement. What I lack is confidence in my own judgment of the situation.

I will have to start at the beginning. There is no need to go into the entire sordid story. He made a profession of faith, but there always seemed to be a cloud over it—a question of sorts. He refused to testify, did not read his Bible except sporadically, did not seek the company of Christian friends or go to church.

I do not know exactly what happened. All I can do is relate the results which are exciting to both Penny and me, even though I am somewhat fearful that we will waken and find them a wonderful dream. I'll try to list these things in chronological order.

1. He asked forgiveness of his mother and me for all the heartache he has caused us throughout the years.

2. He asked forgiveness of a man who has apparantly hated him for the past ten years. And not all the fault was Craig's, although he made the first move.

3. He asked the doctor's forgiveness for all the trouble he caused him while he was drinking.

4. A daughter of one of our friends brought some flowers to him. He thanked her profusely, told her how beautiful the flowers were and asked her to thank her folks for sending them. She came home and asked her mother what had happened to Craig, that he was so different.

5. He sent a note of thanks to two men who did a favor for him. This was the first time I had ever known him to thank one of them for anything. He now thanks the nurses for what they do for him.

6. His copy of the Bible is on the stand by his bed with a number of markers in various places, indicating he is reading the Word of God.

7. He talked with a friend of his about righting some of the wrongs he had done.

8. Dianne came up to see him three times during the last week or so. The last time she was in the room

for twenty minutes or so and stood holding his hand. He didn't start to pressure her about coming back to him, nor did he try to get her to do anything for him.

9. He is suddenly concerned about his indebtedness. He had me call two men he owes money, telling them he will pay them as soon as he can.

He also asked me about other Christian men who used to have terrible reputations as rounders. The implication seemed to be that he wanted to know whether it would be possible for him ever to assume a position of respect in the community.

We want to thank you again for your concern and your prayers. We have felt from the beginning that this illness has been of the Lord. Indeed, we have not been able to pray for his recovery apart from recognizing that God may have caused the illness. At any rate, we want His purpose worked before Craig is restored to health, whatever that purpose may be.

All our prayers as you continue to serve Him wherever you are.

> CORDIALLY IN HIM,
> ROYCE LAWSON

During the next few days Penny was with Craig constantly. He asked her to read his mail, write letters for him, and rub his back and his legs with lotion. He talked with her about Dianne and Stephanie and their plans for the future.

"God has done so much for me," he said, "that I don't think I could ever be happy doing anything except serving Him."

"That's wonderful." Penny looked away quickly to keep him from seeing the tears in her eyes.

"I've been thinking about talking to Dr. Benson about helping in his organization or seeing Pastor Jerry at the mission in Omaha. There are a lot of things I could do around a place like that."

"I'm sure of it." Her voice broke.

Only that afternoon Dr. Morgan had called Royce in to tell him that Craig was steadily growing weaker.

"Would it do any good to take him to Rochester?"

"I've checked his X rays with my son who's specializing in cardiology at Mayo's," Dr. Morgan said. "Their diagnosis confirms mine. However, I'd be happy to make arrangements for you to take him there if that's what you'd like to do."

Penny and Royce talked it over at the dinner table and decided to get Dianne's opinion that night.

"If she agrees, we'll get a plane to fly him to Rochester in the morning."

But God had other plans for Craig. His condition seemed to be unchanged when Dianne went home at the close of visiting hours that night, but shortly after midnight Dr. Morgan had the nurse call them to the hospital. Before they reached his room, he was gone.

"I did everything I could for him," Dr. Morgan said wearily, "but I couldn't keep him alive."

Royce and Penny stared at each other, for the moment unable to grasp the full portent of what had taken place. There were no tears. They would come later, after the shock began to ebb.

"You'll have someone make the arrangements for us, won't you?"

"Of course," the doctor said.

And then Royce and Penny were out on the sidewalk in front of the hospital, the darkness about them as thick and impenetrable as their grief.

"We'll have to go and tell Dianne," Penny said.

"Tonight?"

"She has a right to know."

They called her first and told her they were coming over. She had dressed and was waiting for them in the living room. The pain in her taut young face revealed the fact that she had already sensed the reason for their visit.

"It's Craig, isn't it?"

219

"He died a few minutes ago," Royce told her, angry with himself that he had no gentle way of breaking the news.

She swayed and almost fell. He caught her and helped her to the divan. Mercifully, tears came and Penny took her in her arms, comforting her. At last she stopped crying.

"There's something I have to tell you," she said.

"Yes?"

"I didn't want to tell you until Craig was out of the hospital, but we had decided to go back together."

Royce gasped.

"The last two weeks would have been the happiest time of my life, except for my concern over Craig. You can never know how wonderful it was to go into his hospital room and read the Bible and pray with him. I know now what life with him as a Christian would have been. God gave me a glimpse of it before He took Craig home."

After a time Royce got to his feet.

"I've got some phone calls to make," he said, "so I think we'd better go. Would you and Stephanie like to come with us?"

"Not for a while." Tears came back to her eyes. "I'll come later, but I'd like to be alone for a while."

In the car Royce spoke again; bitterly. "I can't see how God could do this to us! All these years Craig lived for the devil. Then he became a Christian and he and Dianne were going back together and what happened? It isn't just!"

"Royce! We can't doubt God or His wisdom."

"All these years we prayed without an answer. Now he only lives a few short days after he made his decision for Christ. It makes me wonder whether God cares about us or not."

"You know He cares about us," Penny said quietly, trying to quiet the pounding of her own heart.

"Do I?" Bitterness gave his voice a harsh, brittle edge. "Nothing has happened to make me know He cares!"

They were almost home when Penny spoke again.

"I have been praying that if Craig wasn't going to get well enough to be able to live a normal life or if he wasn't strong enough to live a consistent Christian life that God would take him home."

It was as though Royce didn't hear anything she said.

The funeral was different than any that had ever been held in Glenville. Because of Craig's friendship with Pastor Jerry he was asked to come out from Omaha and have a part in the service. Rev. O'Conner spoke first, reading the obituary and telling about the change he observed in Craig's life.

"I'm not going to tell you that Craig lived a good life. That would make a mockery of everything we believe and preach. We often talk about the new life that God gives to those who choose to walk with Him. In this young man we have seen that new life demonstrated dramatically. In his last few weeks on earth he showed us all a transformation that is impossible apart from God."

Pastor Jerry was even more blunt.

"I don't suppose it's generally known," he said, "but Craig came to see me often over a period of eight or nine months. He was tortured by the drunkenness and adultery in his life, but was unwilling to give God full control. Every time I talked with him I was disturbed because I knew that while I was going to heaven he was on his way to hell." Jerry paused and his face beamed. "But now I'm still down here and, praise God, Craig is in heaven. His wasn't a death-bed decision made under the weight of fear. Up until the last day of his life he was planning for the future, looking forward to the day when he would be well enough to leave the hospital and go out to serve God."

Royce reached over and took Penny's small, trembling hand. As the two men spoke, his own anguished railing against God quieted. He began to understand. It was God's mercy and loving-kindness that had prompted Him to let them see the change that had come over Craig. And, with the understanding, all the hurt and bewilderment vanished. It wasn't that he had suddenly fathomed any more of God's reasoning in taking Craig home now, when he had just accepted the new life Christ provided for him. What Royce understood was that he had been wrong in the way he looked at this thing that had taken place. He was no longer angry and hurt that God had taken Craig home so soon. Instead, he was thankful that God had not permitted their son to die before answering their prayers for him.

He bowed his head and silently asked forgiveness for his own lack of faith that God's way was best. The grief was still there, but now it was tempered with joy and peace. His son was in heaven, but before he died the divorce that had been such a cancer to Royce and Penny became a divorce in name only. Dianne was with them, assuming her rightful place as a member of the family. They had much to thank and praise God for.

At the cemetery Craig's friend Larry came up to Royce, eyes glazed with tears.

"I've never heard a funeral service like this."

"We can praise God that Craig's life was changed to make it possible."

Larry lingered there, fumbling for words.

"The last time I was at the hospital to talk to him he tried to tell me what happened to him, but I couldn't dope it out."

"It's really very simple, Larry. I'd like to talk to you about it some time."

"Would you?" Larry's eyes gleamed. "Would it be all right if my wife and I come over some night soon?"

Penny spoke up quickly. "Why don't you come tonight?"

Larry studied her grief-etched face. "Tonight?"

"I don't know of a better time," Royce added.

They were still standing there when Dr. Benson came up to offer his sympathy.

"But you have much to be thankful for. Your son was gloriously and triumphantly converted."

"Yes," Royce answered. "God answered every prayer we ever offered for Craig in all the years we've been praying for him, except one."

"Which one was that?"

"We prayed that He would restore Craig's body and make him well."

"But he's answered that prayer too," Dr. Benson said

222

quietly. "Craig's body has been restored, and he's in heaven now waiting for you."

Royce put his arm about Penny's waist. Tears trickled down their cheeks, but they were not merely tears of grief. There was joy and peace in them.

God was good!